08 JUL 1999

Good Practice Guide to
Maintenance Cost Forecasting

COVENTRY UNIVERSITY

THE HOUSING CORPORATION

Published by Coventry University Enterprises Ltd,
Priory Street, Coventry, CVI 5FB.

First Edition 1999

© Coventry University Enterprises Ltd and
the Housing Corporation

Designed by Anthony Godber

Printed in Great Britain by Reynolds Press
Printers Limited

ISBN 0 905949 73 0

The publisher makes no representation, expressed
or implied, with regard to the accuracy of the
information contained in this book and cannot
accept any legal responsibility or liability for
any errors or omissions that may be made.

A catalogue record of this book is available from
the British Library.

Contents

Foreword   4

From Roger De La Mare, Director of Regulation, The Housing Corporation

Why this guide?   5

The development of the guide   7

Section A: Developing and implementing strategies for maintenance cost forecasting   10

Stage 1: Developing a strategy for maintenance cost forecasting   11

1.1 Making sure the strategy integrates with the organisation's Business Plan   11
1.2 Linking asset management and re-investment strategies to maintenance cost forecasting   12
1.3 Identifying who should be involved in the development of forecasts   13
1.4 Defining terms   14
1.5 The effect of improvements   15
1.6 Finding out about stock condition   15
1.7 Establishing the times scales for forecasts   18

Stage 2: Implementing the maintenance cost forecasting strategy   19

2.1 Building flexibility into forecasting   19
2.2 Checking and fine-tuning forecasts   19
2.3 Prioritising planned maintenance work   20
2.4 Deciding how you will procure maintenance work   20

Stage 3: Linking the work you do on maintenance cost forecasting to other current issues for RSLs   21

3.1 The Housing Corporation's performance standards   21
3.2 Best Value   23
3.3 Energy efficiency   23
3.4 Information technology (IT)   25

Section B: Choosing and using techniques   26

Stage 1: Establishing your cost forecasting profile   27

4.1 Building up the forecasts   27
4.2 Setting time scales and reviewing the forecasts   27
4.3 Incorporating planned and unplanned maintenance   28
4.4 The techniques   28
4.5 Cost forecasting profiles   29
4.6 How to find your cost forecasting profile   31

Stage 2: Applying the techniques   33

5.1 Historical costing   33
5.2 Zero-based budgeting (ZBB)   36
5.3 Life-cycle costing   38
5.4 Attribute surveys   48
5.5 Defect scoring   52
5.6 Quinquennial and regular inspections   59
5.7 Strengths and weaknesses of current techniques   64

Appendix A: Summary of Action Points   66

Appendix B: Case studies   69

Appendix C: References   87

Computer disk (in pocket wallet)   inside back cover

Foreword

From Roger De La Mare
Director of Regulation, The Housing Corporation

Registered Social Landlords (RSLs) cannot rely upon significant grant funding to maintain and repair their housing stock. They must make adequate financial provision for these future costs largely from their own resources. The first step is for them to have an appreciation of what these costs are likely to be. For this reason the Housing Corporation commissioned this guide to help RSLs forecast their future maintenance costs. It is intended for all RSLs, large and small, and contains general principles and practical advice.

The guide has been prepared after extensive consultations with RSLs of all sizes, including the staging of three, well attended, workshops around the country to discover current practice and future needs. RSLs have shown considerable initiative in this area, but have also encountered difficulties. All appreciated the opportunity to get together to talk over the problems. We gratefully acknowledge the assistance of those who attended, and all others who have helped in the preparation of this guide.

No one should pretend that maintenance cost forecasting is easy. Many factors must be considered and there are many uncertainties that can upset the reliability of the forecasts produced. The are several techniques available but these are often presented in a way that is confusing and complicated to put into practice. This guide sets out stage-by-stage guidance so that RSLs can achieve sensible cost forecasts, recognising the realities and pressures in housing organisations today.

I believe that the guide will be of real and practical help to every RSL and other social landlords and I commend it to your careful thought and action.

Roger De La Mare
Chair of the Steering Committee

The project steering committee

Roger De La Mare
The Housing Corporation

Judith Harrison
The Housing Corporation

Tony Cox
The Housing Corporation

Alastair Jackson
The National Housing Federation

Doug Edmonds
Consultant

The project team

Keith Chapman
Head of Building, Coventry University

Gurdev Singh
Research Fellow, Coventry University

Roger Downham
Research Fellow, Coventry University

Martin Beck
Principal Lecturer, Coventry University

A donation from Orbit Housing Association Ltd toward the production of this guide is acknowledged.

Why this guide?

Purpose of the guide

This guide will help you to:

1 Understand the key principles involved in maintenance cost forecasting.

2 Relate the need for maintenance cost forecasting to other current issues for RSLs.

3 Review the range of maintenance forecasting techniques currently available.

4 Decide on the most appropriate forecasting techniques for your organisation.

5 Set up and maintain a maintenance cost forecasting system.

It is aimed at all registered social landlords whatever their size or nature of their stock. Its main audience is the director, line manager or other person with strategic responsibility for maintenance. It should also be of interest to housing management, finance and development staff, chief executives and board members who want to increase their understanding of this very important subject.

▼▼

The importance of maintenance cost forecasting

All RSLs should now be acutely aware of the need to improve the quality of their maintenance cost forecasting.

▼ From a maintenance perspective: future requirements have to be identified and planned for, to ensure stock is lettable and that standards meet landlords' statutory maintenance obligations.

▼ From a financial perspective: cash has to be available when it is required to meet identified maintenance needs. The RSL's rental stream, its other income, its borrowings and investments have to deliver this cash at the right time. An accurate maintenance cost forecast will provide a sound basis for investment planning, treasury management and assessing future rent levels.

▼ From a development perspective: accurate forecasting of future maintenance costs is a critical factor in assessing the viability of new schemes. Development teams also need feedback on component durability when deciding on specifications for new schemes.

▼ From a housing management perspective: letting and managing well maintained and desirable properties is much easier and more cost effective than trying to do the same with poor quality stock.

- From a tenant perspective: all tenants want to live in well maintained and desirable homes and feel confident they will stay that way.

- From a community perspective: one landlord's poorly maintained stock can blight a whole community. Lack of confidence in a landlord's commitment to delivering future maintenance programmes will have a similar effect. Accurate maintenance cost forecasts are an essential ingredient of successful community regeneration projects.

- From a strategic perspective: RSLs need to make best use of existing stock to protect the value of their asset base, guarantee their rental stream and assist them meet future housing demand. Strategic decisions on asset management – whether to maintain, sell, demolish or convert will rely on accurate forecasting.

- From a business management perspective: business plans are essential for business development and must be supported by accurate cost forecasts.

- From a Best Value perspective: good quality maintenance forecasting helps to make best use of scarce resources.

- From the funders' perspective: private lenders will want to be satisfied that RSLs have funded plans in place to protect the future value of assets used as security against loans.

- From the Housing Corporation's perspective: performance standards require all RSLs to 'identify, plan and make adequate financial provision for the repair and improvement of their stock'.

The complexity of maintenance cost forecasting

It would be foolish to pretend that maintenance cost forecasting is a simple business. If that were the case all RSLs would already have effective systems which delivered forecasts appropriate for their circumstances – and you would probably not be reading this guide!

Forecasting maintenance costs for housing stock is a complex issue. Costs are affected by:

- different types of stock – the most common types of stock owned by RSLs overall are purpose built, traditional build, low rise flats and terraced houses but individual RSLs may own very varied stock types including system built, high rise, conversions and maisonettes.

- different ages of stock – on average, 80% of RSL stock is post-1945 and a substantial percentage is less than ten years old. This is consistent across sizes of RSLs and locations. However, an individual RSL may own stock with a very different age profile. For example, it may have a substantial number of Victorian or pre and immediate post-war properties. For these older properties, the date and standard of any rehabilitation work already undertaken will have a significant impact on future costs.

- location of stock – there is a variety of factors associated with location. Maintenance costs are higher in some parts of the country; costs are likely

- ▼ to be affected by the level of stock dispersal throughout an area; the desirability, or lack of it, of a particular location will also affect costs.

- ▼ type of client group - different clients tend to cause different patterns of wear and tear on properties. This will affect the durability of components chosen and the length of time components will last. For example, you would not expect fixtures and fittings to last as long in a scheme for young single people as you would in a sheltered elderly scheme.

- ▼ tenancy turnover rates - higher than average turnover rates, particularly where these are associated with a relatively high level of abandonments, will also tend to increase wear and tear.

- ▼ rising standards and expectations - replacing like with like will often be inappropriate. Higher specifications will tend to lead to higher costs.

In spite of the acknowledged complexity, however, we hope you will find this guide offers an easy-to-use approach to maintenance cost forecasting.

The development of the guide

We began work on the guide after extensive consultations with over 150 RSLs of varying sizes and types, working in different parts of the country. Details of these consultations are contained in the Project Report, available as a companion to this guide from Coventry University (see the References in Appendix C at the end of the guide). We wanted to find out what work they were already doing on maintenance cost forecasting, the difficulties they were experiencing and the help they wanted to improve their systems.

It was clear from the discussions that a prescriptive approach to the guide was not required. The wide variety in the location of their operations, in the type and age of the properties that they own or manage, in their tenant populations and in their management structures and priorities suggested that one method of maintenance cost forecasting, suitable for all, would not be appropriate. RSLs need to use methods appropriate for their individual circumstances.

Some RSLs were content with their existing systems - you may be too. If so, the guide should provide a good practice reference point and act as a stimulant to further development and refinement of your systems.

The vast majority of RSLs, however, wanted to improve their systems. In particular, there was a clear desire to extend the time periods over which forecasting is carried out and improve the accuracy of forecasts. RSLs wanted to see a guide that was concise and practical which was accessible to technical and non technical readers, with alternative forecasting methods clearly explained, backed up by detailed case studies.

Armed with this information we have:

▼ reviewed available technical and social housing sector literature to identify current good practice (the most useful sources are included in the References in Appendix C).

▼ made sure that our approach fits with the financial framework in which RSLs operate.

▼ consulted with other agencies involved in this area such as the National Housing Federation, Chartered Institute of Housing, Housing Centre Trust and the Almshouse Association.

▼ consulted with the Housing Corporation to ensure our approach fits with its regulatory framework.

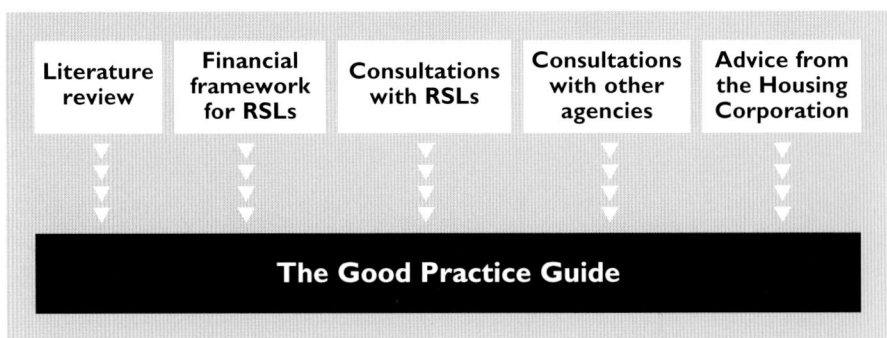

How to use the guide

> ☞ **Action Point**
> ▼▼▼▼▼▼▼▼▼▼▼▼▼
> **All RSLs should read and apply this guide.**
>
> *A summary of all these action points is included in Appendix A.*

Each section of the guide can be read independently, or it can be worked through sequentially as both an introduction to the subject and a checklist for practical action. Throughout the guide 'action points' are highlighted in boxes. An example of an action point box is shown on the left.

The guide is divided into two sections:

Section A
Developing and implementing strategies for maintenance cost forecasting – identifies the strategic factors that RSLs should consider. It examines how maintenance cost forecasting links with current issues affecting RSLs and highlights the management processes needed for successful implementation.

All RSLs will find this section useful, since the basic principles are the same for all, whatever their size or circumstances.

Section B
Choosing and using techniques – helps RSLs identify and use techniques that will assist them with maintenance cost forecasting. The techniques are described in detail and there are worked examples to explain their practical application.

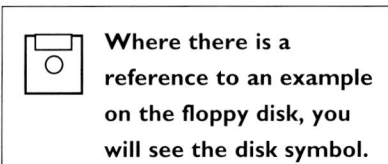
Where there is a reference to an example on the floppy disk, you will see the disk symbol.

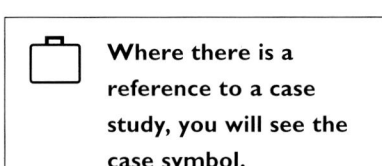
Where there is a reference to a case study, you will see the case symbol.

You will find further examples on the floppy disk which accompanies the guide inside the rear cover. The disk also gives you the opportunity to try out the techniques for yourself.

Appendix A
Action Points - contains a summary of the action points mentioned in the main text of the guide.

Appendix B
Case Studies - contains selected in-depth case studies drawn from the group of RSLs included in the consultation exercise. The case studies demonstrate how a variety of types and sizes of RSLs have tackled maintenance cost forecasting and what they have learnt in the process. References are made to specific case studies at key points in the main part of the guide.

Appendix C
References - a listing of key documents and sources of information on maintenance cost forecasting that are referred to in the guide. A more complete bibliography is contained in the Project Report, available as a companion to this guide from Coventry University (see the References in this appendix).

Section A
Developing and implementing strategies for maintenance cost forecasting

This section identifies the factors that RSLs should consider when developing and implementing strategies for maintenance cost forecasting. It examines how maintenance cost forecasting links with other current issues affecting RSLs and highlights the management processes needed for successful implementation.

Stage 1
Developing a strategy for maintenance cost forecasting

1.1 Making sure the strategy integrates with the organisation's Business Plan

Developing a forecasting strategy in isolation from your organisation's Business Plan will severely reduce its effectiveness. The figure below shows how maintenance cost forecasting fits into a cycle of activity which links the key elements involved.

Stock Condition

The first key element is knowledge of current stock condition. This provides an essential base point from which to start the forecasting exercise. A detailed explanation of how to undertake a stock condition survey is beyond the scope of this guide but 1.6 below identifies some key general issues and Section B recommends particular forms of stock condition survey for cost forecasting purposes.

Long term Forecast

The second key element is the maintenance cost forecast itself. Section B will help you identify the best way to do this depending on the size and type of your organisation. The forecast will provide essential information on future stock requirements needed to make key decisions in the Business Plan.

Business Plan

The third key element, the Business Plan (usually covering a five year period), will be formulated from a wide variety of investigations including the maintenance cost forecast. The forecast will help in making key decisions about:

- organisational goals to be achieved during the period of the Business Plan
- asset management policy and strategy
- funding requirements
- treasury management policy and strategy
- rent levels during the period of the Business Plan

Detailed information about the business planning process is beyond the scope of this guide. Further reading is identified in the References in Appendix C.

Annual Operational Plan

The fourth key element, the annual operational plan, provides a more detailed breakdown of the work to be done in that year of the Business Plan. It will include the programme of planned maintenance for the year based on the maintenance forecast.

Annual Budget

The final key element, the annual budget, will include funding for the planned maintenance programme and for unplanned, responsive maintenance.

Once the planned maintenance programme for the year has been completed and the pattern of unplanned maintenance occurring during the year has been assessed, stock condition records can be updated and the cycle begins again. This process is ongoing throughout the life of the RSL.

> **☞ Action Point**
>
> You will need to make sure that the work you are going to do on maintenance cost forecasting is properly integrated into your organisation's existing business planning system. This will need agreement from the senior management team and ultimately from the Board. They will need to understand how this important cyclical process works.

1.2 Linking asset management and re-investment strategies to maintenance cost forecasting

RSLs need to adopt a strategic view to improve the return from, and increase the value of, their property portfolios. An RSL may find that it has stock:

- in poor physical condition
- in areas that are unpopular because of social, economic or environmental factors
- that no longer fits with identified housing need
- that no longer meets customers' expectations

> **📁 Case study**
>
> ▼▼▼▼▼▼▼▼▼▼▼▼▼
>
> Case study 1 **Touchstone HA: The introduction of an asset management strategy** (see page 70)

As part of its asset management and reinvestment strategies it may choose to:

▼ do nothing

▼ undertake patch repairs

▼ undertake a major refurbishment programme

▼ demolish and rebuild

▼ sell

It will choose one of these options or a combination of them after considering a wide variety of issues. These will include factors relating to sustainable communities, community regeneration, partnership working with local authorities and other agencies, and meeting the requirements of the Housing Corporation. Its ability to choose appropriately will depend significantly on the quality of the maintenance cost forecasts it has available.

> **☞ Action Point**
>
> ▼▼▼▼▼▼▼▼▼▼▼▼▼
>
> You will need to make sure that the work you are doing on maintenance cost forecasting links to any existing strategies on asset management and reinvestment.

It is therefore essential that the reinvestment strategy, asset management strategy and the maintenance cost forecasting strategy link together. This integrated strategic approach enables RSLs to take a much more holistic view of the management of its property portfolio and make sounder business decisions.

If you would like to know more about asset management and reinvestment the References in Appendix C give some further reading.

▼▼▼

1.3 Identifying who should be involved in the development of forecasts

Our consultations with RSLs showed that in the larger RSLs professional maintenance staff developed short, medium and long term maintenance cost forecasts. In smaller RSLs forecasting was often done by finance managers or other managers without a professional maintenance background.

> **☞ Action Point**
>
> ▼▼▼▼▼▼▼▼▼▼▼▼▼
>
> You will need to seek agreement to adopting a bottom up approach to maintenance cost forecasting which involves both maintenance and finance staff in developing and reviewing the forecasts.

Many RSLs used a 'bottom up' approach, with forecasts and budgets being generated from front line staff upwards rather than being imposed by more senior management. Cost forecasts were usually refined and finalised by a team including both maintenance and finance staff. This team then met periodically to review and update the forecast.

We believe that this bottom up approach involving both maintenance and finance staff in the development and review of the forecasts is most likely to give an effective result.

▼▼▼

1.4 Defining terms

It is important to be clear about what maintenance is and what it is not. The definition of maintenance used in this guide is:

'The process of providing building services to the components of housing units to enable them operate at satisfactory levels appropriate to their age, current legislation and Housing Corporation Performance Standards'

In this definition, 'building services' may mean either:

▼ the complete replacement of components eg installing new window units

▼ the refurbishment of components eg repairing and repainting the existing window units

The 'components' involved may be large or small, for example a complete roof or a single tile.

The definition acknowledges that all maintenance work must conform to current standards at the time it is carried out. This means that some measure of improvement is often involved in so called 'maintenance' work.

It is important to note that no mention is made in this definition of the cause of the maintenance requirement. It may be because a component has reached the end of its useful life, but it may equally well be that the maintenance need has arisen because of damage, or misuse, or to remedy deficiencies in the original development work. A maintenance cost forecast must include all maintenance work, whatever its cause. For this guide, the issue is that the work must be done, not why it needs doing. There are other guides that offer advice on identifying needs and actions in this area. For example, 'Safe as Houses' by Crime Concern (see Appendix C - References).

The definition includes all work required, irrespective of how the original component was funded or how the work needed will be funded. RSLs may choose to split their forecasts into different sections to reflect different funding sources eg provisions for future maintenance on rented schemes, or sinking funds for asset replacements created from depreciation contributions in service charges.

Maintenance is either planned for or it is not. In the guide we have followed standard practice in defining these terms:

▼ unplanned maintenance - including responsive maintenance of any kind, whether paid for by rents or by service charges, for tenants or for leaseholders.

▼ planned maintenance - including cyclical maintenance, annual servicing, major repairs, whether paid for by rents or service charges or from reserves and provisions, for tenants or for leaseholders.

Case study

Case study 2 **Collingwood HA: The difficulties in realising the full benefits of an active planned programme** (see page 72)

Action Points

1) You will need to agree the terminology and definitions used within your RSL. This will involve discussions with finance, development and housing management staff.

2) Once the terminology and definitions have been agreed you will need to ensure that your manual and IT systems reflect the changes. This is likely to include reviewing coding systems for maintenance expenditure and scheme appraisal systems. You will need to do your own careful check to ensure that changes are worked through all the organisation's systems.

1.5 The effect of improvements

Very few maintenance programmes are carried out without some measure of improvement being built into the specification to comply with changing legislation, technological developments or rising resident expectations.

Changing requirements may bring forward the end of a component's useful life. For example, emergency alarm systems for the elderly which consist of a flashing 'help' sign outside the building to alert passers-by are no longer considered acceptable and are being replaced, even though they may still work and even though they are cheap to install and maintain.

Components reaching the end of their useful life should not automatically be replaced by identical components. The opportunity should be used to review whether or not something different is required.

In short term cost forecasts the improvement factor can be built in relatively easily. Specifying and pricing specific schemes should include a review of component standards and suitability. In medium to long term forecasts identifying the improvement factor will become progressively more difficult as future changes become harder to predict.

The improvement factor may either raise or lower maintenance costs. For example, making existing buildings more energy efficient tends to involve significant capital expenditure but there can be a long term pay back in revenue costs. Improvement may decrease costs as technological developments in materials and components reduce prices in real terms; or it may increase costs - when entirely new components have to be installed and maintained, such as a carbon monoxide alarm.

> **☞ Action Point**
>
> You will need to ensure that your forecasting system includes an improvement review mechanism particularly for short and medium term forecasts.

1.6 Finding out about stock condition

Good quality information about the current state of the stock is a pre-requisite for good quality maintenance cost forecasting. Properly conducted stock condition surveys and inspection programmes will provide this information.

We consulted with RSLs about how they established the condition of their stock. They identified the following problem areas.

▼ There was often significant pressure to carry out a stock condition survey quickly which meant there was little or no time to consider carefully the required outputs and outcomes.

▼ The stock condition survey itself had often been set up as a stand alone activity, not undertaken as part of a business planning system as shown above. This made it difficult to make effective links between the survey, long term plans and work programmes.

▼ Many RSLs had commissioned a survey without establishing clear aims and objectives and, in consequence, were disappointed to find that the results did not provide them with what they wanted, even where the survey itself had been done to a high professional standard. In particular, the question of how the data would be updated was often forgotten and standard terminology was not agreed.

▼ Even when RSLs felt they had tried to specify what they wanted, they sometimes found that the consultant did not seem to understand their business and was more interested in providing the information the consultant felt was appropriate rather than what was asked for.

▼ On occasions, organisational expectations of the survey had been unreasonably high. It had been seen as the complete answer to all the RSL's maintenance management problems. In some cases poor procedures were used to collect the data and RSLs lacked confidence in the quality, consistency and accuracy of the information produced, particularly where it seemed to contradict their own in-house knowledge of the stock.

▼ RSLs had experienced difficulty in using the survey data collected and applying it to maintenance planning. Problems arose with surveys that were too complex and so comprehensive in the amount of detail collected that they were self-defeating. The sheer volume and depth of information made it impossible to develop workable maintenance programmes.

▼ Often survey data were presented in an inappropriate format. Usually this was because RSLs did not have the necessary computer software to manipulate the data or keep it updated. This problem was compounded where the RSL's IT system and the IT system used for the survey were fundamentally incompatible.

It was evident that, in general, RSL's experience of stock condition surveys was disappointing - an exercise which gave poor value for money. You may well be satisfied with your stock condition survey method. If so, please feel free to skip the rest of this section. However, if your experiences are similar to those of the RSLs we consulted there are a number of publications on stock condition surveys listed in the References in Appendix C at the end of the guide which you might like to read. On the whole, these publications had not been extensively used by the RSLs in our survey. They had tended to rely on the professional expertise of the surveyor they had used. We think the publications do provide useful guidance.

Although this is not a guide to conducting stock condition surveys, we have included some key good practice pointers because effective surveys are so important.

Deciding who should do the survey

Good stock condition surveys require expertise and time to plan, specify, supervise and execute the survey. If you decide to do the survey entirely in-house you will need to make sure you have the expertise and time to do all the stages effectively. If you decide to outsource any or all of the stages you will need to investigate carefully the skills and abilities of the consultants available.

How much stock to include in the survey

The number of units and their diversity of type are the two key variables in deciding on whether to survey the whole stock or to rely on a sample. At one extreme, a small RSL with diverse stock types should consider a 100% survey. At the other extreme, for a large RSL with a limited range of stock types, a sample survey of 5–10% of the properties would produce useful data. Findings from the sample are then extrapolated to reflect the condition of the whole of the stock.

The obvious reason for doing a sample survey is that it represents a considerable saving of time and money compared to a survey of the whole stock. Extrapolated results from sample surveys will not accurately mirror the characteristics of the whole stock. There will a degree of error in the extrapolation which will reduce, by and large, as the sample survey size and range increases. If the sample is not constructed properly to reflect the makeup of the stock the savings will prove to be a false economy. Remember too that the results of a sample survey are fine as a basis for forecasting costs but will not provide sufficient information for detailed cost estimates.

If you are not familiar with sampling techniques then you should get professional advice.

Specifying stock condition surveys

A weak specification is often the reason why RSLs are disappointed with their survey results. It is important to clarify the brief with the surveyor at the outset of the work. The extent of the detail to be collected can vary greatly; a dwelling house could be assessed by a simple survey of its major elements ie roof, walls, doors, windows, or at the other extreme the survey could be much more detailed; roofs would include details of roof coverings, flashing and soakers; walls could include painting, finish, flashings; doors could include locks, hinges, material, finish.

Deciding where your RSL fits on this continuum is critical. There are three major factors to consider:

1 How wide a variety of stock you have - if you have lots of different stock types, collection of data down to too detailed a level will overwhelm you with so much information to manipulate that it will never be used and the effort of collecting it will be wasted.

2 The history of problems in your stock - if your maintenance records show particular problems with roofs, say, then you may well need to collect more detailed data on this building component.

3 The level of materiality - even large scale failure of a small, cheap, easy to replace and relatively non-critical component is not going to materially affect the future wellbeing of the organisation.

Get independent professional advice if you are not sure how to specify the survey.

> **☞ Action Points**
> ▼▼▼▼▼▼▼▼▼▼▼▼▼
>
> If you are planning to do a stock condition survey for the first time or you want to review the way you currently do them, you should:
>
> 1) Read up on the subject using the References in Appendix C in this guide as a starting point.
>
> 2) Speak to colleagues in other RSLs about their experiences and learn from them.
>
> 3) Ensure you give sufficient time to planning the survey before you start to do it. It will save you time, money and grief if you do.
>
> 4) Make sure the planning team is led by someone with maintenance expertise but includes people with IT skills as well.

Manipulating the data

Before you begin the survey you will need to think through how you are going to manipulate and use the data you collect. Improved information technology can help RSLs handle effectively much more comprehensive surveys than previously, but only if the IT database which will be used is specified correctly at the outset. The choice of database software will influence how data is collected, manipulated, used and updated. If the software does not interface effectively with existing IT systems used in your organisation you will find it difficult to use the data for maintenance cost forecasting.

You will need to involve your RSL's IT specialists when you specify the survey.

Executing the survey

Once underway, surveys will focus on assessing the condition of components. The words used to define condition must be clear, understood and consistently applied by all the surveyors taking part. For example, what do words like 'good', 'fair', 'poor' and 'average' mean in the context of the assessment? Surveyors will need to be trained in any grading system used before starting the survey.

Being realistic about what a survey can achieve

A survey provides a 'snap-shot' of stock condition at a particular point in time, nothing more, nothing less. It cannot be the panacea for all your maintenance requirements or dictate future maintenance planning.

▼▼

1.7 Establishing the time scales for forecasts

> **☞ Action Point**
> ▼▼▼▼▼▼▼▼▼▼▼▼▼
>
> You will need to agree the time scales you wish to adopt for forecasting at senior management team and Board level.

You will need to conduct maintenance cost forecasts over a range of time scales. We suggest you undertake forecasts over three different periods of time:

▼ a long term forecast over a 30 year period – this will feed into long term financial forecasts to demonstrate to the organisation, to funders and to other stakeholders such as the Housing Corporation that the organisation can meet its commitments over the period of major loans.

▼ a medium term forecast over a 5 year period – this will feed into the Business Plan to help inform goals and strategies for the medium term development of the organisation.

▼ a short term forecast over a 1 year period – this will feed into the annual operational plan and budget.

As the time scale shortens the level of detail included in the forecast and its degree of accuracy will need to increase. A long term forecast will largely be a desktop exercise using techniques covered in Section B of this guide. The medium term forecast will tend to be based on a form of stock condition survey. The short term forecast will use the stock condition survey data updated by inspection reports on specific groups of properties which you intend to include in planned maintenance programmes that year.

▼▼

Stage 2
Implementing the maintenance cost forecasting strategy

2.1 Building flexibility into forecasting

Forecasts are not one-off exercises. They need to be revised and updated over time. Long term forecasts will need to be revised as more accurate projections become available. Medium term forecasts will need to be revised as annual operational plans are implemented and evaluated. Emerging external factors, which might be financial, economic or regulatory, may also require the projections to be revised.

Forecasts are only a guide to when works programmes will be required. Decisions to activate work programmes to repair or replace components should be timed as closely as possible to the time when component failure will occur so that maximum component life is achieved but without jeopardising the safety of residents and the structural integrity of the property.

The forecast life of a component can only be an estimate. Actual components in a particular group of properties may last for a longer or shorter period of time than the average. Analysis of unplanned maintenance work undertaken will help to establish when this component failure is beginning to happen. Make sure, however that you do not rely totally on tenants' reports of component failure. They may not notice, or be aware of the significance of, tell-tale signs that component failure is imminent or has happened.

> **Action Point**
>
> You will need to set up a system to review and revise long, medium and short term forecasts to ensure that they reflect changing external factors and up-to-date knowledge of stock condition.

2.2 Checking and fine-tuning forecasts

You may well be starting to develop cost forecasting without an extensive property database about components in your own stock and how they have performed over time. In these circumstances you will have to rely on information from other sources about how components in general perform when you are building up your forecast. This information can be found in several of the sources mentioned in the References in Appendix C.

Over time, however, you will be able to use out-turn results and component and cost information from your own stock in your projections. The use of these out-turn results in future forecasts will personalise the forecasts so that they reflect more precisely the environment in which you operate, your client base and your property types. This in turn will improve the accuracy of your forecasts.

You will only be able to do this if your organisation has an effective process for capturing and recording information about components in the stock and how they have performed over time. The information will need to be stored in an easily accessible and user friendly way.

> **Action Points**
>
> 1) You will need to set up a property database and a system to keep it up-to-date. To do this effectively you will need to work with your RSL's IT expert and the development team. They will have a key role to play in providing information about new schemes.
>
> 2) You will need to ensure that your forecasting review process builds in the use of out-turn results so that your forecasts become more personalised to the RSL's own circumstances over time.

2.3 Prioritising planned maintenance work

Although ideally the forecasted maintenance need for resources will always be met, in reality the cost of forecasted maintenance activities may exceed available resources, especially if maintenance backlogs exist. If this is the case there will be a need to minimise, cancel or postpone work programmes. It is important to have an agreed system for prioritising programmes and it is preferable to agree this in principle before you need to use it in practice. Heads are not always at their clearest and most logical when urgent budget cuts are needed!

Whatever prioritisation system you adopt it will need to take account of:

▼ safety - will the safety of residents and other members of the public be put at risk if the programme is delayed?

▼ health - will the delay increase health risks to residents?

▼ function - will there be unexceptable loss of function if the programme is delayed?

▼ aspect - will the asthetic appearance give cause for concern?

An effective system also needs to take into account the cost of postponing maintenance activities. Works which, if delayed, will rapidly increase in cost with time should have priority over works where costs do not increase as rapidly with time. A method of work prioritisation on the basis of performance loss and cost growth as a result of delayed maintenance is examined in Section B - Defect scoring.

> ☞ **Action Point**
> ▼▼▼▼▼▼▼▼▼▼▼▼▼
>
> **You will need to agree a system for prioritising planned maintenance programmes at senior management team and Board level.**

2.4 Deciding how you will procure maintenance work

Whilst this guide does not specifically cover the commissioning phase of maintenance, procurement strategies can have a significant impact on the cost of maintenance. The choice of procurement method has the most significant impact on short term forecasts but will have some impact on medium term forecasts too. Most RSLs consulted aimed to achieve a level of accuracy of between 5% and 10% for medium term forecasting which they felt was adequate for business planning purposes. This margin of accuracy could be significantly be effected by the procurement route chosen.

For long term forecasts there are other more significant variables than procurement method which will affect accuracy.

Traditionally it has always been good practice to tender competitively for building works but there are other options including:

▼ negotiated rates or contract costs

▼ design and build contracts

▼ partnering agreements

If you want to find out more about commissioning maintenance work we have identified further reading in the References in Appendix C.

> ☞ **Action Point**
> ▼▼▼▼▼▼▼▼▼▼▼▼▼
>
> **You will need to review your current methods of procurement and assess the impact of the methods you choose on your short and medium term forecasts. You will need to get agreement at senior management and Board level to changes in procurement strategy.**

Stage 3
Linking the work you do on maintenance cost forecasting to other current issues for RSLs

3.1 The Housing Corporation's performance standards

The Housing Corporation publication 'Performance Standards' sets out the minimum standards in nine key areas that are expected of all RSLs. These standards were introduced on 1 April 1998 and form the basis of the Corporation's regulatory regime for RSLs. The following standards are particularly significant for maintenance and maintenance cost forecasting:

Repairs, long-term maintenance and improvement (Standard I)

RSLs should:

- maintain their housing stock in a reasonable and lettable condition
- identify, plan and make adequate financial provisions for maintenance and improvement works
- provide a responsive repairs service which meets their legal and contractual obligations and which is efficient and effective.
- ensure probity and value for money in these activities

> **☞ Action Point**
>
> You will need to develop a clear statement of what standard of maintenance your RSL believes will achieve this 'reasonable and lettable condition'. Arriving at this definition will involve discussion with applicants, residents and housing management staff to agree what is necessary and affordable. This standard will need to be agreed at senior management and Board level.

Rents (Standard D)

RSLs are required to set aggregate rent levels which are appropriate to their financial and other commitments. Subject to this constraint, the Corporation advises RSLs to restrict their overall stock rent increase to a guideline limit set by the Corporation. This is currently RPI (Retail Price Index) plus 1%.

Special arrangements apply to Large Scale Voluntary Transfers (LSVTs) depending on the date of transfer. If your RSL is an LSVT you should check the Corporation's advice that applies to you.

Information to and consultation with residents including opportunities for participation and influence (Standard G)

RSLs should provide all residents with summaries of current policy and procedures relating to maintenance especially:

- who is responsible for different types of repairs
- methods of reporting and dealing with emergencies
- what tenants can do if the landlord fails to meet its repairing obligation
- planned maintenance and improvement programmes, including cyclical decorations of external and common parts
- alternative or short term accommodation, home loss and disturbance payments and the effect on rents for residents displaced as a result of major works.

> **☞ Action Point**
>
> Rents are a major source of income to fund future maintenance work. These restrictions on rent increases will affect your RSL's ability to fund future programmes. You will need to assess the impact of this change on your forecasts. If the rent increase restrictions affect your organisation's ability to meet essential future maintenance commitments you will need to alert the senior management team and the Board. Your RSL may then wish to raise this issue with the Corporation.

RSLs should consult residents, in ways in which meet residents' wishes, about maintenance and improvement plans and the implications of those plans for residents.

RSLs should provide residents with reasonable opportunities to participate in and influence the design and management of maintenance services. These opportunities should be reported to residents at least once a year and they should be consulted on them from time to time.

Risk management (Standard C)

RSL Boards are required to manage prudently the organisation's financial affairs and the risks it faces. Effective plans and forecasts to meet future maintenance commitments are an essential tool to enable this prudent management of finances and risk.

To comply fully with this performance standard, RSLs are expected to undertake a risk assessment exercise for all their business. Risk assessment and the subsequent management of the risks identified involve three main stages. Each of these stages will affect maintenance cost forecasting.

Stage 1 - Identify all potential risks
Various risks arise within the area of maintenance cost forecasting. These include:

- economic variables, such as interest rate changes, material price or labour rate fluctuations
- new or improved health and safety requirements and regulations
- future rent setting and capping policies
- changes in government policy
- poor quality stock condition information
- poor quality forecasting techniques
- rising customer expectations

RSLs need to identify the likely risks in all these areas.

Stage 2 - Control risks by removing, reducing, avoiding, transferring or accepting risks
Responsibility for controlling risks should be delegated to the most appropriate post holder. For example the maintenance manager may be responsible for controlling risks associated with maintenance cost forecasting.

Stage 3 - Carry out regular risk reviews or appraisal exercises
This process needs to be done on an annual basis.

> **☞ Action Point**
>
> 1) Maintenance cost forecasting is part of your maintenance policy and procedure. You will need to provide residents with information about how you do it.
>
> 2) You will need to involve residents appropriately in the long, medium and short term planning process for maintenance.
>
> 3) You will need to ensure that risks associated with maintenance cost forecasting are included in the risk management exercise.

3.2 **Best Value**

During the time this guide has been developed the government has introduced the concept of Best Value. The Best Value Framework will seek to ensure that the services of the RSLs are of high quality, focused on meeting the aspirations of their residents and represent cost effectiveness in delivery. The Housing Corporation has completed a consultation exercise with RSLs about how Best Value should apply in practice. Guidelines will be published during 1999.

It is likely that RSLs will not be compelled to adopt Best Value. However, they will be encouraged to move beyond the minimum performance standards to bring their performance up to that of the best. In this way performance standards and Best Value are intended to complement each other.

The Best Value Framework will encourage RSLs to seek to improve continuously their performance year-on-year. Performance on service delivery should be regularly monitored through the use of performance indicators and compared by benchmarking results against those of other similar RSLs. The use of customer feedback on the services and the development of imaginative and innovative ways of involving tenants in the work of the RSL is a key feature of Best Value.

Mechanisms to encourage Best Value will include:

- statements by RSLs on the level and range of services that are to be provided to residents
- reports by RSLs on the level of performance achieved
- comprehensive organisational reviews of service delivery by RSLs
- downward pressure on costs, in part through comparative assessments
- extensions to the current performance indicator regime
- Best Value pilots by RSLs
- surveys of Best Value activity
- the publication of comparative RSL performance indicators (PIs)
- the further development of PI and benchmarking clubs

It is clear that Best Value in practice will evolve over time as ideas develop and in the light of shared experiences.

> **Action Points**
>
> 1) **You will need to keep up-to-date with Best Value as it develops nationally and make sure you are aware of how your RSL is developing and implementing Best Value internally.**
>
> 2) **If you are seeking out best practice on maintenance cost forecasting, using it to improve the way you forecast maintenance costs and you are involving residents in the process you are already demonstrating Best Value techniques.**

3.3 **Energy efficiency**

Improving the level of energy efficiency in an RSL's stock benefits:

- residents – in lower fuel bills and warmer, healthier, more comfortable homes
- the RSL – properties are easier to let, there are fewer repair problems since a high level of thermal insulation is the most effective method of preventing condensation and there are fewer tenant complaints

▼ the environment – with reduced gas (particularly carbon dioxide) emissions and less use of finite resources

A significant number of RSLs have already taken steps to develop and implement energy efficiency policies. These should establish:

1 Targets for minimum energy ratings per unit
2 Targets for giving energy advice to residents
3 Requirements to carry out energy audits
4 Training programmes for staff and residents
5 Specifications for new build, refurbishment, planned and unplanned maintenance work
6 Time scales for achievement of targets
7 Performance monitoring
8 Evaluation and review mechanisms

The Home Energy Conservation Act 1995 (HECA) requires housing authorities to not only promote energy efficiency in their own stock but also to prepare a report identifying practicable and cost effective energy conservation measures likely to significantly improve the energy efficiency of all homes in their area. Local authorities are charged with the responsibility of establishing a baseline, setting targets and priorities, and monitoring and evaluating progress. Performance standards advise RSLs that they should assist local authorities in meeting their energy efficiency commitments via their planned programme.

RSLs ideally should include an energy audit component in the surveys and inspections they undertake to produce costed plans for future planned maintenance and improvement programmes. In practice, however, this is not always possible as the skills required for conducting an energy audit and a stock condition survey are different. Where separate surveys are conducted, the data will need to be collated to enable cross referencing of information. In February 1999, People for Action produced a mechanism for measuring progress on energy efficiency. This is contained in 'Energy Management for Sustainable Warmth – A Guide for Registered Social Landlords', see the References in Appendix C.

It has been demonstrated that including energy efficiency measures in work programmes often has only a marginal effect on costs and opens the door to a wide range of potential sources of funding such as the EC SAVE programme and the EC THERMIE programme.

If you would like further information about this you should contact the Department of the Environment, Transport and the Regions (DETR) about their energy efficiency best practice programme or look up the References in Appendix C at the end of this Guide.

☞ **Action Points**

▼▼▼▼▼▼▼▼▼▼▼▼▼▼

1) You will need to incorporate any agreed energy efficiency targets in your forecasts

2) You will need to ensure that the results of energy efficiency audits are used to inform the forecasts you prepare.

3.4 Information technology (IT)

Many of the techniques that will be identified in Section B are suitable for computerisation. Some depend on IT for their full execution. At one extreme, IT applications may be the use of a PC based spreadsheet program for forecasting life-cycle costs, at the other, the introduction of a comprehensive maintenance management package interfacing with development, housing management and finance. Many software houses now produce IT packages which include forecasting maintenance costs. If the advertising by software companies were to be believed, RSLs would merely need to purchase the package and all their problems would be solved. Reality, however, is somewhat different!

Decisions about the use of IT are complicated. There are many conflicting factors. It is beyond the scope of this guide to provide a comprehensive evaluation of IT options for maintenance. You should get professional advice if you need to undertake a major review. There are, however, some key points to consider in relation to maintenance cost forecasting:

▼ do you need IT at all? - very small RSLs can use the recommended techniques without the use of IT

▼ using PC based packages - small RSLs will find that standard office programs are more than adequate for the recommended techniques

▼ stock condition records can be kept on a simply constructed database - this should allow for key data to be manipulated and analysed in a variety of ways to help in decision making

▼ spreadsheets can be used to calculate forecasts

▼ interfacing maintenance cost forecasting with existing IT systems - there are many off-the-shelf and bespoke software packages around in the social housing sector but, although the situation is beginning to change, few have well developed property data base, maintenance planning and cost forecasting programmes.

If your RSL's IT system is lacking in this area you may find it easier to download data from a main-frame system to a PC database and spreadsheet programme which you can configure yourself. This will, however, have the major disadvantage that the forecast and plan will not feed back into the main frame programme. Updating will then become difficult and will probably not be done at all. The alternative is to investigate the possibility of adding in a planning and forecasting programme to the existing programme. Even if this is possible, it can often be prohibitively expensive.

Your RSL may be in the process of upgrading its IT system. If so, it is very important that current and future requirements relating to a property database, maintenance planning and cost forecasting are incorporated into the specification for the system. This guide should give you lots of ideas which will have implications for an IT specification.

☞ Action Points

You will need to:

1) Invest some time in getting to grips with IT so that you can contribute effectively to organisational discussions. This applies whatever the size of your RSL.

2) Analyse your needs thoroughly before you invest in a system.

3) Allow plenty of time to discuss requirements and agree a specification - however long it is, it is unlikely to be wasted.

4) Allow for future change. Do not think that today's answer will hold firm for ever.

5) Be clear about what data you wish to hold, what data is fixed and what data will change. Remember that your existing data, in whatever form, is valuable.

Section B

Choosing and using techniques

This section helps RSLs identify and use techniques that will assist them with maintenance cost forecasting. The techniques are described in detail and there are worked examples to explain their practical application.

Stage 1
Establishing your cost forecasting profile

We have identified the set of techniques that we think are likely to be most useful in building up cost forecasts for your RSL. We have called this your RSL's 'Cost Forecasting Profile' (CFP). We now explain how you go about building up your forecasts and then go on to explain how to choose your RSL's CFP.

4.1 Building up the forecasts

You will need to go through three stages to build up a maintenance cost forecast:

▼ First, you will need some knowledge of the condition of your stock.

▼ Second, you will develop a maintenance plan for the period that you want to forecast.

▼ Third, you put costs to this plan.

This three stage process is the same in principle whether you are making a long, medium or short term forecast and whatever techniques you use to assist you.

4.2 Setting time scales and reviewing the forecasts

In Section A we suggested you should aim to cover three time scales in your forecasts:

▼ short-term, which will be effectively the annual forecast,

▼ medium-term, which will coincide with the Business Plan (normally for a five year period)

▼ long term, which we suggest should cover a 30 year period to link with your RSL's financial forecasts for its loan repayments.

Clearly the levels of accuracy that you can achieve will decline as the time period is extended. What is important is that all three forecasts should be consistent with each other and that they are each updated annually to reflect changing circumstances. This review should take place as part of the annual Business Plan review. If this is carried out systematically, the forecasts will, at any time, represent the best opinion about future costs and will be available immediately for all those who need it.

4.3 Incorporating planned and unplanned maintenance

Maintenance cost forecasting needs to include all the maintenance costs associated with your stock. This means that both planned and unplanned maintenance must be included. For the short and medium term it will be easy to split costs between planned and unplanned. For the long term, the breakdown will be much more uncertain.

Even if your RSL intends in the long term to reduce the proportion of unplanned maintenance it undertakes, there will always be unpredictable maintenance costs to meet. These will include earlier than expected component failure, vandalism and costs associated with property turnover. To forecast these costs you should use historical or zero-based costing techniques, coupled with analysis of the causes of unplanned maintenance and an assessment of likely future trends.

4.4 The techniques

There is a variety of techniques available to help you develop your maintenance cost forecasts. These techniques do one of two things. They either help you make better estimates of condition and maintenance priorities in your stock, or they help you predict costs. They vary from sophisticated life-cycle models to simple reworks of historical data. They are described briefly now:

Stock condition surveys
Stock condition surveys can be used for a variety of different purposes including preparing maintenance cost forecasts. We have recommended two specific types of stock condition survey in this Section; attribute surveys and defect scoring systems. Section A gives guidance about conducting general stock condition surveys in 1.6.

Historical cost forecasting
This method uses previous costs as a basis for assessing future costs. It is used mainly for short term forecasts to calculate the amounts to be spent in the coming year on planned and unplanned maintenance.

Zero-based budgeting
This method starts from a nil cost base and considers all activities and programmes as if they were new. It takes a questioning attitude to maintenance expenditure and asks if priorities and objectives have changed rather than simply following through what happened before.

Life-cycle costing
Life-cycle costing is concerned with predicting failure patterns of elements or key components so that financial provision can be made for long term maintenance.

Attribute surveys
Attribute surveys allow RSLs to predict medium and long term repair costs across the whole of the stock on the basis of reliable data. It is similar in principle to life-cycle costing analysis.

Defect scoring
Defect scoring is a standardised building inspection system. It grades component failure in the short to medium term in order to ensure that repair and replacement activities are largely undertaken at the time they become necessary.

Quinquennial and regular inspections
Quinquennial (five yearly) inspections are designed to detect faults that need rectifying and identify those areas of work that must be carried out to prevent problems occurring in the future. The five yearly cycle is supplemented by regular inspections. This approach is mainly applicable to smaller RSLs.

4.5 Cost forecasting profiles

We have said that the Cost Forecasting Profile (CFP) is the set of techniques that is most likely to be useful to your RSL in the development of its maintenance cost forecasts for the short, medium and long term time periods. This does not mean that you should be restricted to these techniques, but we consider they have the best chance of success under particular circumstances. We have tried to identify what those circumstances are. Two factors are particularly important and they are the ones we have used in recommending which techniques you should adopt:

1 Size of the organisation
The size of the organisation is the first key determinant of the CFP. The greater the size of the RSL the more likely it is that it will benefit from computerisation and already has experience of manipulating large amounts of maintenance data. It is likely to have sufficient resource capability for survey work and be able to employ specialist technical staff.

2 Method for updating stock condition records
The method the RSL uses to update its stock condition records is the second key determinant of its CFP. The RSLs we spoke to used both periodic and rolling updates of stock condition. Both of these options can provide stock condition information as a basis for satisfactory cost forecasts. However, some techniques lend themselves more readily to periodic updates rather than rolling programmes.

Our investigations identified possible advantages and disadvantages to both methods. The quality of data obtainable from periodic updates should be better than from rolling programmes. With periodic updates there should be better briefing of consultants and in-house staff and more likelihood that the process will be tendered. Data should also be controlled more effectively.

However, periodic updates are expensive. They provide valid condition assessments for only a short time period and the evidence suggests that they can be badly executed.

Rolling programmes are a cost-effective means of keeping stock records up-to-date where they can be attached to a planned (cyclical) maintenance programme, but in some cases they can present problems of commitment and implementation.

There are other factors which have some effect on the best choice of techniques but these are less critical than the two above:

Whether or not your RSL is an LSVT organisation

Under agreed transfer arrangements, LSVTs already have costed maintenance and improvement programmes for their stock. The principle of establishing accurately assessed future maintenance costs based on stock condition should be continued as good practice, following the expiry of the conditions of transfer arrangement.

Location of stock

In some areas, particularly in urban and inner city locations, high turnover and void levels with difficult to let properties will distort the balance between responsive and planned maintenance. Normal component life cycles can be radically shortened and a far greater proportion of maintenance will be undertaken responsively. The unpredictable nature of damage will almost certainly mean that forecasting the overall maintenance cost from year to year will be much more difficult. You will need to use your own local knowledge to assess likely life-cycles in any forecasting method used.

Type of client group

In the same way that location will vary the balance between planned and unplanned maintenance, so will the range and type of client group housed. Again, you will need to use your local knowledge to determine the particular effect of your client groups on the life-cycles of components and the likely proportion of planned to unplanned maintenance.

Degree of computerisation

The number of components that a building is divided into and the amount of stock will generally dictate the extent to which computerisation will be needed. All the forecasting techniques described will benefit from the use of at least a spreadsheet application, but particularly life-cycle costing and attribute surveys. It should be possible for the smaller RSL to use the defect scoring method without the use of a computer.

Type of stock

Some types of stock make the wholesale application of certain techniques more viable. For example, where there is a relatively high degree of standardisation of components, sizes of units and type of properties, life-cycle costing can be more easily applied.

4.6 How to find your cost forecasting profile

To find your recommended CFP, follow these steps:-

Step 1: What size is your RSL?
We have divided RSLs into four size categories:

▼ Large: RSLs with more than 3000 properties

▼ Medium: RSLs with between 500 and 3000 properties

▼ Small: RSLs with between 20 and 499 properties

▼ Very small: RSLs with less than 20 properties

'Properties' mean the number of separate buildings and this total will give an approximation for the purposes of deciding your CFP.

Step 2: What is the main way you update your records of stock condition?
RSLs in practice often use a combination of the two methods (periodic and rolling) for updating stock condition records. You need to decide which is your major preferred method of updating, irrespective of whether or not you use the other method from time to time.

Step 3: Select your Cost Forecasting Profile (CFP)
Depending upon the size of your RSL and your main method of updating your stock condition information, select your Cost Forecasting Profile for short, medium and long term planned maintenance forecasting from the following table:

Size of RSL	Very Small	Small	Small	Medium	Medium	Large	Large
Method of updating		Periodic	Rolling	Periodic	Rolling	Periodic	Rolling
Short-term	5 & 1	4 & 1	4 & 1	4 & 1	4 & 1	4 & 1	4 & 1
Medium-term	5	3	4 & 1	3	4 & 1	3	4 & 1
Long-term	5	3	2	3	2	3a	2a

The numbers in the table refer to the different techniques recommended for your profile:

Key	Technique
1	Historical costing or Zero-based budgeting
2	Life-cycle costing
2a	Life-cycle costing - Integrated Management System
3	Attribute survey (stock condition)
3a	Attribute survey (stock condition) - Integrated Management System
4	Defect scoring (stock condition and prioritisation)
5	Quinquennial and regular inspections

Why we recommend these profiles

Short term forecasts – very small RSLs should use quinquennial and regular inspections to determine their annual forecasts. All other RSLs should prioritise their maintenance work, using techniques such as defect scoring, and cost it using historical costing or zero-based budgeting.

Medium and long term forecasts – RSLs using a rolling programme to update stock condition records should find it relatively straight forward to use defect scoring to grade component failure, over both the short and medium terms. These RSLs will already have in place a cycle of surveyor inspections on a percentage of the stock per annum. The use of a defect score pro-forma can be combined with this exercise without significant use of extra resources. Life-cycle costing is recommended for long term forecasts for these RSLs as the site based information on the components will be relatively accurate and up-to-date.

RSLs undertaking periodic stock condition surveys will generate data with a relatively short 'shelf life' unless the survey data is combined with a life-cycle component. This life-cycle component is a integral part of the attribute survey technique and allows the projection of cost forecasts over a medium and long term.

Whatever survey method is used it must generate a robust set of data records derived from actual site based inspections. This must be seen as good practice for all RSLs.

Larger RSLs need to consider how best to integrate their cost forecasting models with their existing management information systems. Up-to-date information about component performance and costs should to be fed into the forecasting models once they have been set up. Most of the forecasting models and techniques require a large amount of data which often makes computer-based systems the only realistic option.

Building improvement costs into base maintenance figures
The techniques will provide base maintenance figures only. Some element of improvement is inherent in all maintenance work and must be allowed for in cost forecasts.

For short term forecasts, improvements can be costed on a project by project basis, using normal scheme estimating techniques. You will need to meet current building standards as a minimum. You will also need to consider your customers' views of their homes and seek to meet, if not exceed, their expectations.

In the medium and long term, the improvement element will be difficult to determine. It will depend on a number of variables ranging from technological change, to tenant demand and improving requirements such as HECA. In these cases the raw forecasts should be modified using factors based on past experience. For example, RSLs pursuing a planned maintenance programme for stock in poor condition which suffers from high void/turnover rates and tenant dissatisfaction with the quality of their accommodation should consider a percentage uplift to help redress these problems.

Managing without an extensive property database
You may not have detailed information on component life-spans and replacement costs from your own records. The life-cycle costing techniques can be modified by the use of approximate life-span and cost data. Best estimate data on life-spans and costs will give a reasonable indication of future costs without the immediate commitment of time, money and effort in undertaking a full analysis. Some source data on this is contained in the References in Appendix C.

Once you have decided your CFP, you should move to Stage 2 of this Section for a detailed description of the use of the techniques specified.

Case studies

▼▼▼▼▼▼▼▼▼▼▼▼▼

Case study 3 **Hexagon HA: Rolling updates (see page 73)**

Case study 4 **Downland HA: Periodic condition surveys (see page 76)**

Stage 2
Applying the techniques

Stage 2 takes you through, step-by-step, how to implement the techniques which can assist you in maintenance cost forecasting. Worked examples are included. There are also examples on the floppy disk attached to this guide in the rear pocket. You can use these to practice the techniques for yourself.

The relative strengths and weaknesses of each of the techniques are identified in a comparative table at the end of the Section.

With the exception of historical costing, the methods and examples do not incorporate assessments within the forecasts to account for inflation. Other variables such as interest rates, cost uplifts for improvements, technological change and obsolescence are also excluded. RSLs should monitor and develop indices to reflect the impact of such variables in relation to their own areas of operation. Current day costs are used in the calculations. LSVTs will have initially used the inflation assumptions in their DCF model.

▼▼▼▼▼▼▼▼▼▼▼▼▼▼▼▼▼▼▼▼▼▼▼▼▼▼▼▼▼▼▼▼▼▼▼▼▼▼

5.1 Historical costing

Description
Historical costing is a standard method of forecasting future costs based on the examination of previous costs. Its uses are mainly in the short term, where it can be applied to calculate the amounts to be spent in the coming year on planned and responsive maintenance. The extent to which historical cost information may be used largely depends upon the level of detail of historical maintenance records held by the RSL and the way in which they have been stored.

How to set up the method
There is no set technique for using historical costing to forecast future maintenance costs. RSLs will need to use methods which suits their individual requirements and resources. There are, however, a number of key issues you will need to consider.

You will need to have accurate cost information available on responsive and planned maintenance activities undertaken. For some RSLs it may be necessary to introduce more robust systems for the monitoring and recording their maintenance activities and cost information. Using historical cost forecasting over the long term will be subject to a significant degree of error due to the uncertainty of predicting future variables. Where actual costs vary significantly from cost projections in forecasts it is essential to analyse the reasons for this before using the data for forecasting.

Some RSLs, particularly small ones, use historical cost forecasting to predict responsive and planned maintenance costs for the forthcoming year, by simply applying a factor for inflation to the previous year's costs:

£74,680 × 1.035 = £77, 294
(total cost x inflation figure)

The next level of application would be to average costs over a number of previous years. The number of years selected will depend on evidence of trends or movements that should be projected forward. For example, an RSL with ongoing problems of vandalism over the last two year period without effective preventative steps can assume that this will continue and should be built into the forecast.

It is also possible to incorporate an 'ageing factor'. This is a percentage added to compensate for the fact that as a property grows older it needs more maintenance work to keep it up to standard. The degree of uplift required will be a decision for each RSL and should take into account their own stock knowledge. For example, a stock acquisition by an RSL of a portfolio of ageing (pre 1919) inner-city terraced units, which resulted in a total stock increase of 5% would warrant introducing an additional ageing uplift of, say, 2% to the forecast over and above the stock increase. This would allow for higher costs associated with older properties. This ageing factor could then be revised and refined, as actual out-turn data became available on maintenance costs.

Because changes in stock size can produce inconsistent projections, many RSLs forecast future spending on planned and cyclical maintenance by reference to a cost per property. This figure is obtained by referring to the previous annual cost of each item of planned and cyclical maintenance carried out on a property. These previous costs may be used or alternatively an average taken of previous costs from several years. The cost per property is then multiplied by the number of properties in the stock (or in that year's planned programmes) and multiplied by a factor for inflation, as follows:

Actual yearly cost per property (£)

Item of cyclical maintenance / Year	1994	1995	1996	1997	1998
External painting	420	402	397	460	448
Appliance servicing	81	74	101	95	84
Total yearly cost (£)	501	476	498	555	532

$$\frac{501 + 476 + 498 + 555 + 532}{5} = 512 \times 1.1475^* = £587 \text{ (x inflation factor)}$$

Above: example of the calculation of cyclical maintenance costs based on historical costs per property.
*This is an inflation allowance from the 'average year' of 1996.

Remember that if a planned maintenance programme has been undertaken during the period this will affect the average element cost and total forecast.

RSLs who have in-depth historical cost records can use them to obtain more detailed and more accurate forecasts of future responsive maintenance costs. The procedure is as follows.

1 The first step is to average the amount spent on each building element (or component, depending on detail required) for each year for which records are held. This is done by dividing the total costs for each element each year by the number of that element in the stock of properties that year.

2 These average element costs are then summed and divided by the number of years for which records are held. This gives the forecasted average element cost for forthcoming year.

3 This figure is then multiplied by the number of those elements in the stock to give the total cost for the year ahead.

4 All these costs are added to give a total amount, which is then multiplied by a factor for inflation and a factor for ageing to give the total responsive maintenance cost forecast for the coming year.

The following example illustrates this process. You can practice this approach using the disk included with this guide.

Explanatory notes to the table:

(a) - average amount spent on responsive maintenance of heating systems in 1994 (total amount spent divided by number of heating systems)
(b) - average amount forecast to be spent on maintenance of heating systems in 1999 (sum of the average amounts spent on heating systems from 1994–1998 divided by the number of years involved)
(c) - total amount forecast to be spent on responsive maintenance of heating systems in 1999 (average amount forecast multiplied by the number of heating systems)
(d) - total amount forecast to be spent on responsive maintenance before adjustments made (sum of forecast element costs)
(e) - total amount forecast to be spent on responsive maintenance after adjustments made (amount before adjustments multiplied by a factor for inflation and a factor for ageing)

	Actual average element costs (£)					1999 forecast	
Element	1994	1995	1996	1997	1998	Average element cost (£)	Total element cost (£)
Roofs	398	248	324	296	354	324	16200
Chimneys	245	125	115	192	101	156	7800
Windows	215	345	210	385	154	262	13100
Doors & frames	210	197	146	254	229	207	10350
Plumbing	198	365	298	148	176	237	11850
Heating	367(a)	368	175	246	384	308(b)	15400(c)
Total							74700(d)

£74,700 × 1.1475 × 1.02 = £87,432(e)
(total cost x inflation factor x ageing factor = total responsive maintenance cost forecast)

Above: example of the calculation of unplanned maintenance costs for 50 units based on historical costs.

How to maintain the system

You will need to ensure that you record cost information for maintenance activities accurately. You should ensure that systems are in place to collate and record data on maintenance and repair activities and their associated costs. Depending on the amount of data involved, it may be necessary to use a spreadsheet to carry out the forecast.

The continuing usefulness of the historical cost forecast will depend on how easy it is to incorporate information from site based staff into the cost projections, for example, increased costs because of high security charges, vandalism or rapid stock turnover.

How to use the method effectively

You will need to monitor and review projections to compare actual costs with those forecast. Discrepancies in the forecast should be investigated by examining any significant variations in the actual element cost and the projected figures.

Historical costing is a good method for predicting responsive repairs as trends in costs can be projected over the short term. The method is quick and inexpensive. However, this method is unsuitable for long term projections because of the large number of variables, such as changing maintenance policies, inflation and increasing tenant aspirations. These impact significantly on long term projections. The accuracy of the method is also significantly reduced if it does not reflect local condition assessments.

> **Case study**
>
> Case study 5 **Marches HA: Historical cost forecasting** (see page 78)

5.2 Zero-based budgeting (ZBB)

Description

ZBB is a budgeting technique that assumes that the cost allowed in every item in the budget is zero, until you can justify its existence and show the benefits that the expenditure brings. Its purpose is to create a questioning attitude, so that each activity must be justified in relation to the way it contributes to the objectives of the organisation. Although management accounting techniques like this one are really outside scope of this guide, we include it here because the approach is a useful discipline when thinking of short-term cost forecasting. There is more information on the technique in the References in Appendix C.

Applied to the annual maintenance costs for your RSL, ZBB would mean that your previous year's costs and activities are ignored, and you develop your annual budget from scratch. You have to justify every item of expenditure. You have to take a questioning attitude to the maintenance budget asking if priorities and objectives have changed, rather than simply following through what happened before. You might ask, for example, 'does this item need to be carried out at all?' or 'is there a better way of organising our callout plumbing?'. Whilst such questions are often on the minds of maintenance managers much of the time, this technique forces a justification of the methods you propose to use. Therefore it is a good discipline.

The technique is appropriate for short term forecasts and is particularly useful if your RSL has fallen into bad habits on maintenance! These bad habits might include the use of so called 'contingency sums' in forecasts, lack of analysis of the patterns of spend and lack of thought about future trends. Continuing to use historical cost forecasting in these circumstances will perpetuate past mistakes.

Larger RSLs will find this difficult to apply in its most rigorous form every year because of the sheer scale of the operation. Smaller RSLs should be trying to achieve this anyway, particularly when their budgets are very restricted, because it gives them some firm priorities. We suggest below an example of how you might apply the technique, modified to suit the situation of RSLs.

How to set up the method

We will focus on one possible application by way of an example – the plumbing budget. Remember that the method requires that you will have to justify all the expenditure in your budget against the expected benefits to your RSL. Using the method, you should carry out the following:

Step 1

Divide all the items in the plumbing budget into two types of activities: (these are called 'work packages' in ZBB jargon).

1. The activities that you know you must provide for genuine emergencies and health and safety provision (these are the so called 'base' work packages, because they recognise the minimum level of feasible activity for the RSL in this area).

   You should then identify the different levels of service that you could provide for each package, with each possibility fully costed out and with the benefits of these different service levels clearly explained.

   For example, the cost of providing immediate callout for all plumbing defects, against the cost of a one or two-day callout for non-urgent defects, and what that would mean in terms of statutory obligations, tenant satisfaction and meeting the stated objectives of your RSL.

2. The activities which you know there are some alternative ways of carrying out. An example might be the planned replacement of ball valves in a particular estate (these are called 'alternative work packages' in the jargon – because there are alternative ways of doing them).

Step 2

List all these work packages in order of their importance against the stated objectives of your RSL. For each package, make a very clear statement of justification for every activity against what your RSL is trying to achieve.

Obviously the base decision packages will figure high on this list because of their importance. The process of ranking is very important and senior management should contribute to this. You should also get agreement between maintenance and housing management on this ranking and try to get as much consensus as possible, although this may not always be possible!

The purpose of the exercise is that it will focus your mind, and that of senior management, on more effective ways of delivering the packages of work.

Step 3

You then allocate the budget, giving the minimum funding to each activity that is required to get the jobs done, in the order of agreed priorities and to the agreed service levels.

How to maintain the method

Properly carried out, ZBB should result in a more efficient allocation of resources and more accurate budgets. However, it can be time consuming. Therefore you should consider highlighting certain aspects of your annual maintenance budget each year and treat them to this approach. There would be considerable benefits from this analysis.

Having carried out a questioning approach to the plumbing for instance, other areas can be given a similar treatment. It could be that you focus on a different part of the budget next year. It might be roof repairs, or kitchen replacements. The intention is to subject the budgets to detailed and searching analysis, rather than rolling on the figures from one year to the next.

How to use the method effectively

In practice, you will need to focus on certain aspects of the maintenance budget where there is some doubt about how effectively it is operating or where there might be some changes needed.

ZBB should focus on value for money and makes very clear the relationship between the cost and benefits of different maintenance elements. The questioning attitude must be always in the mind when carrying out the technique. It is a systematic method of challenging the status quo and getting better value for money.

Because it can be time consuming you need the support of senior management and their active participation in the process in order to implement ZBB.

▼▼

5.3 Life-cycle costing

Description:

Life-cycle costing involves predicting the replacement costs of building elements, components or sub-components of housing units to forecast their total long term maintenance costs. The technique relies on accurate predictions about the useful lives of elements and components and the costs of replacing them. In its purest form, the model only accounts for maintenance costs arising from the need to replace components. In the social housing sector this is only part of the total maintenance requirement. RSLs also need to identify maintenance costs likely to arise before replacement, e.g. servicing and repainting costs.

There are many variations of the technique in use. We describe one which attempts to make the model applicable to the circumstances of RSLs.

How to set up the method

The diagram below summarises the main steps involved in setting up a life-cycle model:

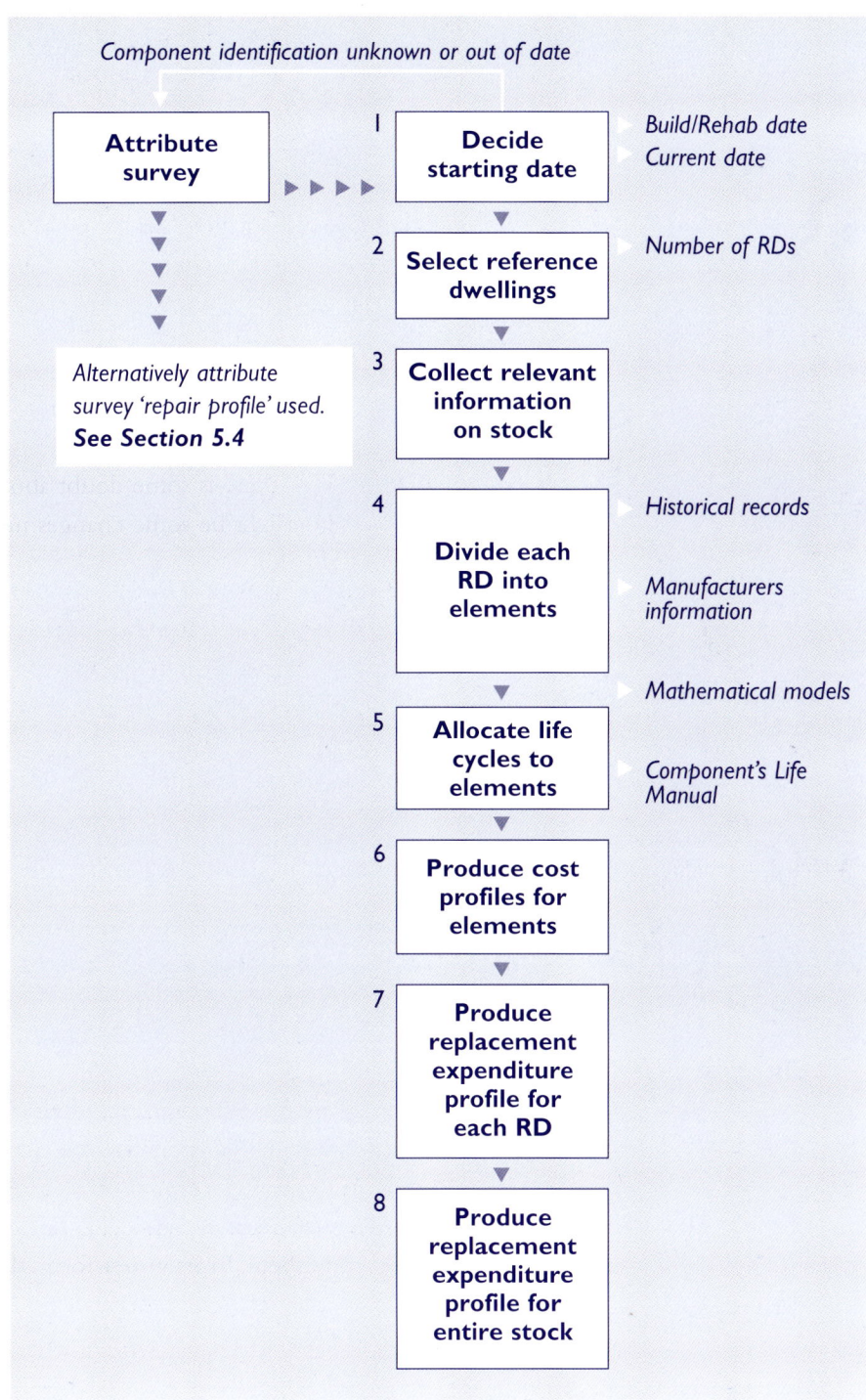

Above: the main steps involved in developing a life-cycle costing model

Step 1

The first step is to decide where the starting point of the exercise is to be and over what length of time the cost assessment is going to take place. The exercise can begin either from the date the properties were first built or rehabilitated or from a recent date when the identification of elements, components and sub-components of the housing units were known. If you are fortunate enough to have accurate information from both sources it would be prudent to incorporate data from the most recent set. In practice most RSLs will rely on recently completed stock condition surveys to provide them with this information.

If the current element and component identification is not known or is out of date, it will be necessary for the RSL to conduct an attribute survey on a sample of the stock in order to obtain the necessary information. The survey will need to link into existing records of design specifications or schedule of works to date accurately some of the components. The use of a freshly commissioned attribute survey will provide a high level of elemental/key component information.

Step 2

The second stage is to select one or more 'reference dwellings'. These should be typical of the RSL's stock. Ideally there should be a reference dwelling for each type of property owned by the RSL to increase the accuracy of the forecast.

Information is required on the numbers and types of different properties, their ages, geographical distribution and any changes to stock through development or sales. It is possible to specify a reference dwelling type to incorporate occupation by certain client groups, such as special needs, so that variations in key component life-spans can be analysed.

Selecting a reference dwelling for each type of property held by an RSL may not always be feasible in practice. In such cases, the focus should be on property types that make up a significant part of the stock portfolio. Accuracy will depend on the amount of time and money available for the exercise so that compromises will inevitably have to be made.

Step 3

The effectiveness of the method depends on the RSL having accurate information on the elements and components for the selected reference dwellings. This information should include detailed component identification, design specifications, and date of installation or replacement. Each attribute or element (such as a roof) is made up of components (tile, flashing) which are in turn made up of sub-component materials (slate/lead).

Step 4

You will need to consider carefully how many and which components to select for each of the reference dwellings. You must include all the components that contribute significantly to maintenance costs.

You will need information about the frequency of component failures and the cost of component replacements. If your association has a well-maintained database, the identification of component life-spans and cost may already be possible. If not, incorporating these extra fields into a database will be a relatively straightforward venture.

The breakdown of component information into sub-components may over-complicate the model and not produce practical benefits in terms of improved maintenance delivery. Planned maintenance programmes to deal with larger component failure will anyway tend to include sub-component replacement, whether required or not.

You will need to have this element/component information in a readily accessible form. The selection of a manageable list of elements (ranging from 15–30) will help in manipulating the data effectively and ensure the outcomes are of real practical use.

If you have recorded historical details of maintenance work for a sufficient time you will be able to incorporate your own component lives into this model. These life spans have the advantage of being specific to your housing stock and will be more accurate as a result. You should seek to develop these as time moves on and refine them in the light of your experience. A systematic and regular way of agreeing component lives amongst all maintenance staff would be a useful approach.

It may also be possible to use manufactures' information and even mathematical techniques to assist in the division of reference dwellings into elements and in assigning lives. Alternatively, there is a variety of published information and data on the life expectancy of building components. These include the 'Component Life Manual' by HAPM (Housing Association Property Mutual), 'Maintenance Cycles and Life Expectancies of Building Components and Materials' by NBA Consultants Ltd and in various publications from the BRE (Building Research Establishment). The usefulness of the 'Component Life Manual' is limited because the lives are cautious 'insurance' values. Workable estimates of components lives are also incorporated in REVKIT a revenue modelling system produced by NFHA (now NHF) software. The tables of lives supplied with REVKIT distinguish between component lives insured under HAPM, and the lives expected under average or high conditions of exposure. These sources are listed in References on Appendix C.

Over the last few years there has been a significant increase in the number of information technology systems available on the market designed to assist the housing professional. LIFESPAN by Property Tectonics is one such system with a particular emphasis on maximising the use of stock condition information. This system enables the preparation of life-cycle generated portfolio maintenance plans, allows users to design their own query features and also offers budgetary fit and works rescheduling facilities.

For costing information, your own knowledge of securing maintenance contracts, commissioning and procurement and elemental replacement costs is the best source. However, the NHF Schedule of Rates and a variety of pricing books on the market can also provide useful information in this area.

Step 5
The next stage is to allocate life-cycles to elements. The most commonly used method of achieving this is to allocate a replacement cost to the year when the average life of the component is reached. For example, a window

costing £1000 has an average replacement life of 30 years. The table and chart below reflects this profile:

Element	Component	Average life	Unit cost (£)	Year					
				10	20	30	40	50	60
Window		30 Years	1000			1000			1000

Note based on present day costs (£)

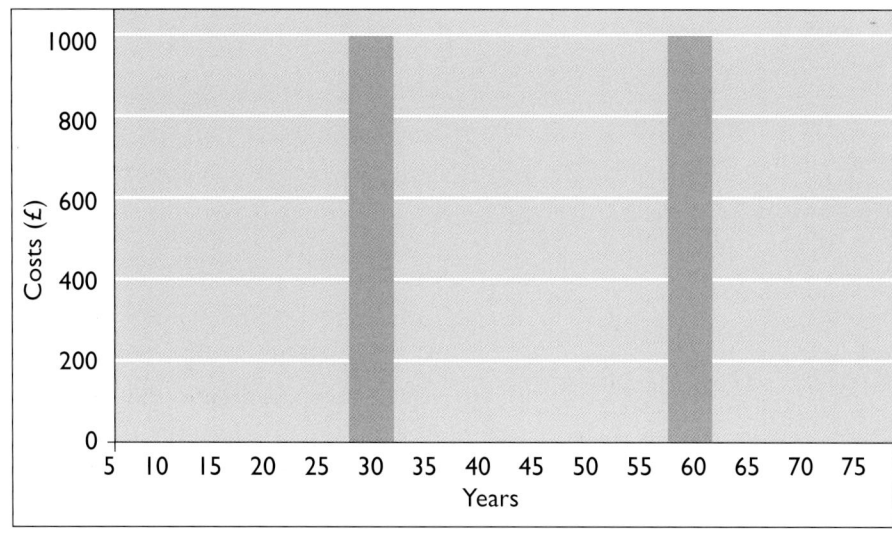

Above: total costs allocated to average replacement year

Step 6

The actual replacement of a component will probably not occur exactly at the average replacement year. Costs for replacement should therefore be distributed or 'smoothed' over the life-span of the component using a normal distribution. This distribution works on the premise that any item's life-span has the most incidence of, in this case failures, around the average year. Incidence of failure falls of uniformly on either side of the average. This gives a maximum life span of approximately 1.5 times the average life span and a minimum of approximately 0.5 times the average. In the above example the window would have a maximum life of approximately 45 years and a minimum life of approximately 15, with the lower probability of failure being around these extremes and the higher probability around the 30 year area. This distribution can be seen in the table and chart below:

Element	Component	Average life	Unit cost (£)	Year								
				5	10	15	20	25	30	35	40	45
Window		30 Years	1000			23	136	341	341	136	23	23

Note based on present day costs (£)

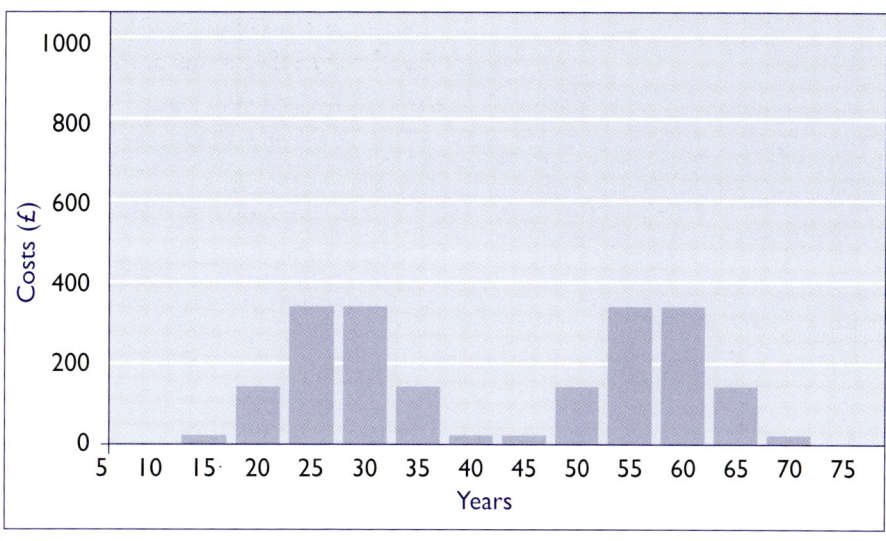

Above: replacement costs 'smoothed' or normally distributed

Step 7

The next stage is to develop a replacement expenditure profile for each of the reference dwellings. This is done by aggregating the expenditure profiles of the individual components of the dwellings to give one profile.

At this stage you should also add in:

▼ cyclical costs for key components that require ongoing servicing or maintenance

▼ an amount to cover overheads directly related to the works programmes such as specifying, tendering and supervising the work. RSLs will often have a standard percentage add on for this, usually around 8%

▼ VAT on material and works costs

The table on page 44 illustrates this stage. You can try out this technique using the computer disk that accompanies this guide.

Step 8

The final stage is to produce a cost profile for the entire stock. If the exercise was undertaken from when the properties were built or rehabilitated, the reference dwellings need to be grouped in specific, usually five year, time bands. These reference dwelling age bands are combined with the expenditure profiles for the reference dwellings to produce a replacement expenditure for the entire stock. For example, a reference dwelling that is 20 years old with a roof decking that has an average life of 40 years will require replacement works in 20 years time.

The table at the top of page 45 illustrates the effect of age banding using a 1979 newbuild (N/B) rehab. reference dwelling.

Element	Component	Average Life	Quantity	Cyclical Cost pa (£)	Replacement Cost (£)	Year 5	10	15	20	25	30	35	40	45	50	55	60
Roof	Roof decking	40	6		65								390				
	Fascia	25	6		22	132	132										
	Roof covering	60	60		20	1200											
	Collar	60	1		50	50											
	Soffits	25	13		10	130	130										
	UPVC downpipe	30			12	12	144	144									
	UPVC gutter	30	9		15	135	135										
Doors & windows	Ext. door frame	35	2	15	50	75	75	75	75	75	75	175	75	75	75	75	75
	Ext. door	25	2	20	250	100	100	100	100	600	100	100	100	100	600	100	100
	Int. door frame	35	8		50							200					
	Int. door	25	8		100					800					800		
	Window	30	6	100 per dwelling	250	500	500	500	500	500	2000	500	500	500	500	500	2000
Plumbing	Bath	30	1		350	350					350						
	Basin	35	1		230							230					
	WC	35	1		250							250					
	Ball valve	15	1		30			30			30			30			30
	Cold water tank	30	1		200						200						200
	Boiler	20	1	50	500	250	250	250	750	250	250	250	750	250	250	250	750
Total component costs						0	0	30	500	1562	2539	780	890	30	1562	0	4109
Cyclical maintenance costs						925	925	925	925	925	925	925	925	925	925	925	925
VAT @ 17.5%						162	162	167	249	435	606	298	318	167	435	162	881
Total overall cost						1087	1087	1122	1674	2922	4070	2003	2133	1122	2922	1087	5915

Above: replacement expenditure profile for a reference dwelling

Element	Component	Average life	1979 N/B or Rehab. Adjusted life	Qnty	Replacement Cost (£)	Year							
						5	10	15	20	25	30	35	40
Roof	Roof decking	40	20	6	65				390				
	Fascia	25	5	6	22	132					132		
	Roof covering	60	40	60	20								1200
	Collar	60	40	1	50								50

If a condition or attribute survey has been carried out to identify the current state of repair of the stock, the yearly costs for each reference dwelling are multiplied by the number of properties that it covers. These totals are summed to give a long-term forecast of total expenditure for the entire stock. An example of total stock profile, based on a survey approach, is given in the table and chart which follow:

		Year									
		2001		2006		2011		2016		2021	
Property type	Number of properties	R.D. cost (£)	Total cost (£)	R.D. cost (£)	Total cost (£)	R.D. cost (£)	Total cost (£)	R.D. cost (£)	Total cost (£)	R.D. cost (£)	Total cost (£)
A	75	450	33,750	285	21,375	1,540	115,500	812	60,900	465	34,875
B	150	784	117,600	1,014	152,100	2,674	401,100	452	67,800	104	15,600
C	40	0	0	65	2,600	385	15,400	468	18,720	942	37,680
D	450	492	221,400	548	246,600	84	37,800	247	111,150	1,864	838,800
E	110	0	0	348	38,280	480	52,800	278	30,580	1,462	160,820
Totals	825		372,750		460,955		622,600		289,150		1,087,775

		Year									
		2026		2031		2036		2041		2046		2051	
Property type	Number of properties	R.D. cost (£)	Total cost (£)	R.D. cost (£)	Total cost (£)	R.D. cost (£)	Total cost (£)	R.D. cost (£)	Total cost (£)	R.D. cost (£)	Total cost (£)	R.D. cost (£)	Total cost (£)
A	75	642	48,150	962	72,150	785	58,875	1,021	76,575	845	63,375	4,022	301,650
B	150	786	117,900	548	82,200	654	98,100	152	22,800	245	36,750	94	14,100
C	40	2,048	81,920	364	14,560	210	8,400	765	30,600	1,115	44,600	3,214	128,560
D	450	1,420	639,000	659	296,550	354	159,300	472	212,400	829	373,050	746	335,700
E	110	968	106,480	482	53,020	642	70,620	1,012	111,320	2,654	291,940	3,248	357,280
Totals	825		993,450		518,480		395,295		453,695		809,715		1,137,290

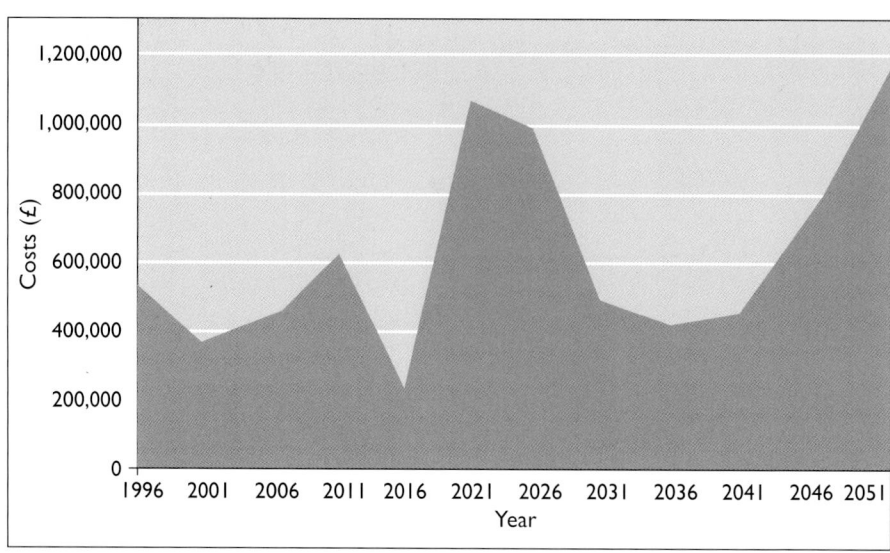

Above: an example of a cost profile for an entire stock

The peaks and troughs within the expenditure profile will cause some concern for the effective delivery of future maintenance programmes as well as to the crucial finance functions of the RSL. However, these variations in cost projections can be readily smoothed to assist in service delivery and cash flow management. Replacement activities can be brought forward or pushed back following actual site based inspections of the components. Also, the relative priority of each of the replacement activities can be reviewed as part of a management decision making process. For example, an RSL's decision to ensure the provision of full double glazing in all units within a specific timescale will impact on the delivering of other programmes.

How to maintain the method

You will need to ensure that there is a system to collate and record data for key component life-cycles and their associated costs. An RSL's own data on life-cycles and component costs will always be more useful than information obtained from published or other sources. Information from future stock condition surveys will be an important source of data.

The use of information technology and spreadsheets will help in setting-up and continuing to monitor and review the projections.

How to use the method effectively

Larger RSLs will need to integrate their life-cycle costing into their management information system. Information on key component life-cycles and out-turn costs from front-line maintenance activity needs to be captured easily and brought into the system. For example, when a job order is raised for component replacement that falls outside the planned programme the information can be used to adjust cost projections.

Life-cycles and costs should be monitored and reviewed regularly to identify and rectify any significant variations. It is possible to test the 'assumed life' data and costs introduced into a life-cycle technique by a carrying out a 'sensitivity analysis'. This can test the overall effects of changes in the base data, for example:

- a change in the applicable VAT rate
- a reduction in all external component life-spans by a percentage factor to reflect extreme conditions
- an increase in the cost of boilers due to changes in health and safety regulations

Alternatively, more specific changes can be tested, such as the introduction of actual out-turn life-span data. This process is important as it allows the RSLs to amend some of the inaccuracies in the base data and enables a greater confidence in the overall method.

You can also examine the 'what if' consequences of using different components. For example an RSL may wish to consider improving the specification of its window replacements. The revised life-cycle, replacement cost and 'cost in use' information can be fed into the model to test out its effects on projected costs.

When linked into condition surveys, this approach can result in the formulation of repair programmes. This is achieved by tracking those components approaching their average life span and introducing a site based inspection system, such as defect scoring (see later) to generate actual works programmes.

The pros and cons of life-cycle costing

Life-cycle costing is a very effective forecasting tool when used for a large number of properties and taken over a long period of time. There are however some problems associated with this technique.

From your own experience, you may well be aware of the wide variations in component life-spans and in component replacement costs. There will also be variations due to economic cycles, methods of procurement and inflation which cannot be forecast with any certainty over a long term time span.

Some RSLs may lack the necessary data about the age and type of property within their portfolio and about the range and type of key components. This data shortage will significantly reduce the usefulness of this technique.

The method makes the assumption that RSLs carry out a whole range of works in a systematic way. When the expenditure profiles are drawn for the first time, the projections of short term works requiring immediate action can be quite alarming. Often components have passed their average life-spans, with those that have already failed being picked up largely as responsive works. Maintenance management policies that propose, often by default, retaining components way beyond their natural lives and picking up any failed items by expensive responsive maintenance need to carefully assess the economic wisdom of this course of action.

> **Case study**
>
> Case study 6 **Threshold Tennant Trust: Life-cycle costing as part of an integrated property management system** (see page 80)

Life-cycle costing projections will need to be revised to take into account economic variations, such as cost of materials, and technological change and obsolescence to ensure continued applicability.

Finally, the requirement for some IT expertise in setting up and maintaining a life-cycle costing spreadsheet may require extra training, or extra IT resources for some organisations.

5.4 Attribute surveys

Description

Attribute surveys combine accurate component identification, obtained through site based inspections, with a life-cycle costing approach. The basic information is obtained from a sample of the stock - see the notes on sampling in 1.6 in Section A. Standard stock condition surveys, even if undertaken by experienced surveyors will only identify the current condition of buildings and make accurate estimates of repairs over a limited time span, whereas attribute surveys enable longer term projections.

We recommend this approach to RSLs who periodically update their stock records. We are encouraging you to carry out these site based inspections to maintain a high level of knowledge of the actual condition of your stock.

How to set up the method

As with all surveys, the first step must be to ensure that the brief is tightly drafted with the focus on achieving specific aims and objectives. Attribute surveys are intended to generate high quality, accurate, site based element and component identification information.

An attribute survey examines the physical attributes or elements of a building. Each attribute or element (such as a roof) is made up of components (tiles, flashing) which are in turn made up of sub-component materials (slate, lead). The number of elements/components recorded in the survey will depend on the diversity of the housing stock, as well as the degree of detail or level of analysis required from the survey. The survey will need to link into existing records of design specifications and schedules of work to accurately date some of the components. Elements and components which contribute significantly to maintenance costs must be included in an attribute survey.

An outline of the main steps involved in an attribute survey is shown in the following diagram:

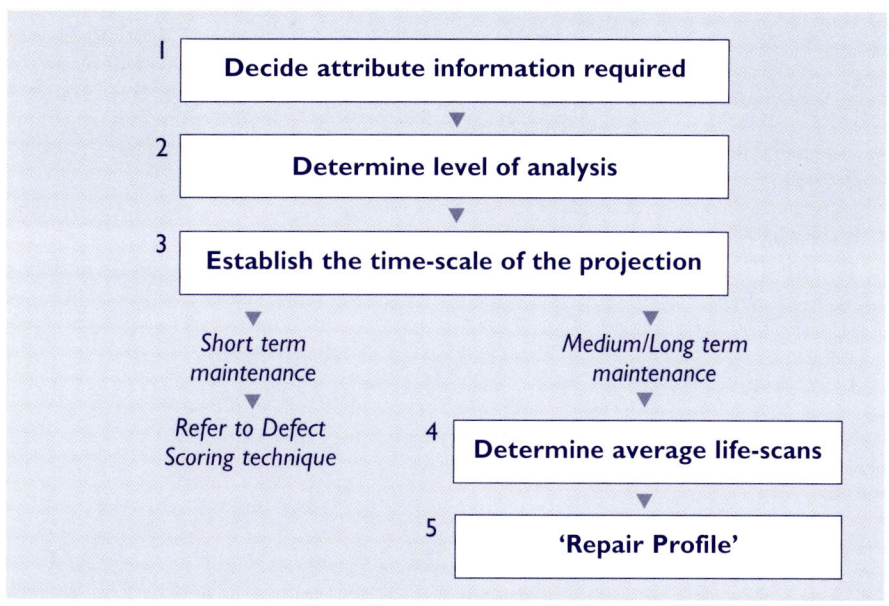

Above: an overview of key steps within an attribute survey

Step 1

You will need to decide the range of attribute information you require to meet your RSL's particular situation but minimum attribute information should include:

- electrical systems
- roof coverings
- rainwater goods
- bathroom fittings
- windows and external joinery
- kitchen fittings
- floor finishes (if provided)
- fabric in common parts (if provided)
- heating and plumbing systems

Step 2

A simple analysis of a roof would note the roof covering material and type of chimney (if present), for example, concrete interlocking tiles and a brick chimney. This information would be adequate to establish future repair costs at a basic level.

For a detailed 'repair profile' it is necessary to list the main components and identify their different service life expectations, for example collecting information about roof components such as the flashing. There are two reasons for collecting detailed attribute and repair information:

- the data can be used to inform the way actual attributes and components perform. The maintenance and development departments need to share this information on component performance so that appropriate decisions can be made about future component choices.

- for commissioning maintenance work.

Step 3

You will need to be clear about the purpose of the survey. Do you wish to use the survey to: carry out catch up repairs, undertake planned maintenance programmes, provide information on the need for future funding, provide information for a more detailed repair plan or to feed information into the development policy or corporate plan?

Assessments can be:
Short term or medium term – You should refer to the defect scoring technique in the next section.

Medium term or long term – For projections over these periods you will need to record details of attributes and combine these with component life information. Attribute surveys provide the detailed attribute and key component information to allow repair profiles (see below) to be constructed.

The decision on which time scale to choose will depend on how far into the future you want to estimate repair liabilities. The further ahead the predictions are made about the future condition of a building the less accurate they become. Long term projections will need to be revisited once the actual rate of component deterioration becomes more apparent. variables such as changing maintenance policies, technological change, inflation, rising tenant aspirations and obsolescence will all have an impact on the accuracy of long term forecasts. Applying defect scoring will assist in bringing the short term works programme into clearer focus.

Step 4
It is possible to obtain life cycle information from manufacturers, published sources or from experience. Manufacturers' information and published sources are averages and as such the data will be subject to a range of error. One of the purposes of establishing repair profiles (see below) is to improve the understanding of the performance of building materials. A variety of factors can impact on expected lives, such as the performance of the component, environmental conditions, usage and maintenance policy. The use of life cycles based on experience provides a more accurate basis for cost projections.

Step 5
Repair profiles allow RSLs to assess building performance and to forecast the costs of future repairs. Repair profiles are the result of combining attribute and component information with repair needs and repair costs at different points in time. Repair profiles are often costed for a building component over a given time span, say 50–60 years.

As a forecasting technique repair profiling relies heavily on life-cycle information. If a sampling strategy is used, it is important to group the stock into property types. These can cover construction types, age, location; can distinguish between new-build or rehabilitated properties and different basic layouts. Section A covers key issues about sampling in 1.6.

Information needs to be recorded on building components for each house type. This includes the average quantity or extent of components, the date they were installed, the average life of the component and its replacement cost. The information can be stored in the following tabular form:

Element/ Sub element	Repair item	Date installed	Quantity	Unit	Rate (£)	Repair cost estimate (£)	Useful life (Years)
Roof/ Structure	Renew sarking felt	1970	5.5	sq.m.	36	198	30
	Renew facia	1970	17.6	m.	15	264	50
Services/ Heating	Renew gas boiler (<150kw)	1985	1	No.	500	500	15

Above: an illustration of attribute information necessary to generate repair profiles

Repair profiles can be expressed in 'property type' tables, in a similar form to the expenditure profiles in life-cycle costing Step 7. Repair profiles for the stock are then derived by selecting the repair profiles for the most appropriate type of property and adjusting in relation to the scheme. Expected repair times are recorded in 5 year bands to assist in the prioritisation of repairs. This banding smoothes the need for repairs over a period of time, allowing the programming of batches of work to be carried out simultaneously.

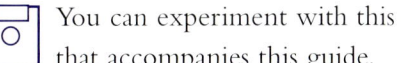 You can experiment with this technique using the computer disk that accompanies this guide.

Whereas the repair profile to forecast repair costs to a single unit is subject to a large margin of error, when considered over a large number of units and taken over the life of buildings a workable prediction of future cost can be made for forecasting purposes.

After conducting an attribute survey, RSLs will be able to link their primary survey data carried out on a sample of their stock into a full life-cycle costing analysis (see Steps 7 and 8 in the section on life-cycle costing). This will allow a replacement expenditure profile for each unit type in the sample survey to be generated as well as an overall replacement expenditure profile.

How to maintain the method

The collation of the data generated will be large and the use of IT and spreadsheets will be in some cases the only realistic option. Such systems will allow the attribute information to be readily accessible and easily updateable. Information about ongoing replacement specifications and costs can be entered at the time of the works, allowing accurate identification of the components and adding to the database of information on stock condition.

The use of IT and spreadsheets can also assist in the ongoing monitoring and review of projections. Whether IT is used or not, it is important that RSLs should record data from key component life-cycles and their associated costs.

How to use the method effectively

The use of an RSL's own data on life-cycles and costs is important in ensuring the most effective use of this technique. Attribute surveys are productive tools for forecasting over the medium and long term as they are based on the condition of RSL's actual stock with the data being easily filtered through into the formulation of repair programmes.

Larger RSLs will need to integrate their attribute survey information into their management information systems. Information on key component life-cycles and out-turn costs from front-line maintenance activity needs to be captured easily and brought into the system. For example, when a job order is raised for component replacement that falls outside the planned programme the information can be used pro-actively to better inform further cost projections.

As with conventional life-cycle costing described above, the life-cycles and costs should be monitored and reviewed regularly to identify and rectify any significant variations. It is possible to test the 'assumed life' data and costs introduced into a life-cycle technique by a carrying out a 'sensitivity analysis' in the same way as described in life-cycle costing.

As with all sample surveys, the sample should be as representative as possible or extrapolation will be inaccurate. Similar weaknesses mentioned in the previous section associated with life-cycle costing are also evident in this approach.

> **Case study**
>
> Case study 7 **Salford HA:**
> **Attribute Surveys**
> (see page 81)

5.5 Defect scoring

Description

Defect scoring is a technique which can be used to identify maintenance priorities. It is particularly suitable for use by RSLs with backlogs of maintenance works. Importantly, it will identify the priorities that exist with a backlog, especially those items of maintenance which fall into 'health and safety' categories.

The method does not require a high level of surveying expertise. Once properly structured basic training has been undertaken, the method can be implemented by any RSL staff member visiting a property to record its condition. Defect scoring aims to overcome the subjectivity and variation that can occur when different people carry out property surveys.

The quality of information obtained from inspections undertaken by different individuals varies because of different:

▼ knowledge about properties, materials, components and factors affecting deterioration

▼ observational ability and experience

▼ commitment to the job

▼ ideas of acceptable and required levels of component performance

▼ prejudices about the effect of occupant behaviour on maintenance problems

A defect score is established by a value analysis. For each building component a limited number of defects is established.

How to set up the method

Firstly, you will need to identify those members of your staff who will be carrying out inspection work. Then, using typical properties, simulated surveys can be undertaken. The aims of this simulation are to clarify understanding of the terms used in completing a defect scoring survey and reach a common view on how the ratings should be applied. Achieving these aims before starting the surveys is critical to the success of this technique.

You will then need to clearly establish what and how many attributes are to be surveyed. As a minimum you will need to survey:

- the roof
- doors and windows
- the external envelope
- the kitchen
- the bathroom
- heating systems
- electrical systems
- drainage

Alternatively, each of these attributes could be broken down into their constituent parts. This decision depends upon your local knowledge of your building stock, its general condition and the elements in which you are particularly interested.

You should keep things as simple as possible. If there are too many attributes, the system will become time consuming and ineffective. No system should be so rigid that it does not allow for any local problem to be picked up on a survey under the heading of 'special element'. The defect score for that attribute can be made known to the maintenance manager for the necessary action to be taken.

Once on site, the attributes to be surveyed are examined and given a score under five separate headings:

1 Gravity - this identifies how serious the defect is, using a rating ranging from 1= extremely serious to 8 = not serious. For example, a roof is observed. If there are a number of missing tiles, loose and missing flashings then a rating of 1 (very serious) would be recorded. If a single tile has slipped a rating of 8 (not serious) would be recorded. Ratings of 1, 2 or 3 are then given a score of 5, ratings of 4 or 5 are given a score of 2 and ratings of 6, 7 & 8 are given a score of 1.

2 Intensity - this category identifies how damaging a defect might be using a score ranging from 1= slight, 2= clear and 4= end stage. For example, do the missing roof tiles mean that water will penetrate the dwelling and cause further damage? If so, then a score of 2 (clear) would be recorded. If the missing tiles are causing a lot of further damage then the roof might be at the end of its useful life and a score of 4 (end stage) would be recorded. If the dislodged tile is unlikely to cause any further damage then a score of 1 (slight) would be recorded.

3   Extent - this category identifies how extensive the observed defect is, with a score range of 1= isolated incident, 2= partial, 5= substantial and 10= everywhere. For example, a large number of dislodged tiles are allowing water to penetrate a number of places over the roof. A score of 10 (everywhere) would be recorded. If, however, the single dislodged tile is unlikely to cause water to penetrate then a score of 1 (isolated) would be recorded.

4   Cause - this category identifies if the defect is caused by its age or if it has been caused by other means. This is important, because if it is age then the component is likely to be at or near the end of its life, whereas if the damage is accidental this may not be so. Therefore a score of 2 = ageing and 1 = other is used.

5   Place - the position at which a component fails can either be critical, meaning it will cause other damage to other components, or may have little effect and cause no further damage. A score of 1= neutral position and 5= critical position. For example, if the missing roof tile will allow water to penetrate and effect the electrical distribution board then a score of 5 (critical) would be recorded. If, however, the missing tile is unlikely to allow the water to penetrate any further than the sarking felt then a score of 1 (neutral) would be recorded.

To illustrate the score method of calculating the defect here are three more examples:

Defect 1 is a pitched clay tile roof with a large number of missing tiles and loose flashings, some tiles have delaminated, there is no sarking felt present and water is penetrating, bringing down the first floor ceiling in a number of areas.

Defect score category	Range of scores	Actual score recorded	Running calculation	Running total
Gravity	1, 2 & 3 = 5 4 & 5 = 2 6, 7 & 8 = 1	Very serious score 2 recorded = 5	5 multiplied by next category	5
Intensity	1 = slight 2= clear 4= end stage	Roof covering at end of its life = 4	5 x 4 =	20
Extent	1 = isolated incident 2 = partial 5 = substantial 10 = everywhere	Defect everywhere = 10	20 x 10 =	200
Cause	2 = ageing 1 = other	Caused by ageing = 2	200 x 2 =	400
Place	1= neutral 5 = critical	Place is critical = 5	400 x 5 =	2000
			Total defect score = 2000	

Defect 2 is at the other extreme; a single clay tile has slipped, sarking felt is present and there is no evidence of damage from water penetration.

Defect score category	Range of scores	Actual score recorded	Running calculation	Running total
Gravity	1, 2 & 3 = 5 4 & 5 = 2 6, 7 & 8 = 1	Not serious score 8 recorded = 1	1 multiplied by next category	1
Intensity	1 = slight 2 = clear 4 = end stage	Slight damage = 1	1 x 1 =	1
Extent	1 = isolated incident 2 = partial 5 = substantial 10 = everywhere	Isolated incident = 1	1 x 1 =	1
Cause	2 = ageing 1 = other	Caused by other factors = 2	1 x 1 =	1
Place	1 = neutral 5 = critical	Place is neutral = 5	1 x 1 =	1
			Total defect score =	1

For defect 3, a more likely scenario, the clay tiled roof has a number of missing tiles but the sarking felt is maintaining watertightness, some tiles have delaminated and some flashings are loose.

Defect score category	Range of scores	Actual score recorded	Running calculation	Running total
Gravity	1, 2 & 3 = 5 4 & 5 = 2 6, 7 & 8 = 1	Causing concern score 5 recorded = 2	1 multiplied by next category	2
Intensity	1 = slight 2 = clear 4 = end stage	Roof covering is in need of attention = 2	2 x 2 =	4
Extent	1 = isolated incident 2 = partial 5 = substantial 10 = everywhere	Defect is substantial = 5	1 x 1 =	20
Cause	2 = ageing 1 = other	Caused by ageing = 2	20 x 2 =	40
Place	1 = neutral 5 = critical	Place is neutral = 1	40 x 1 =	40
			Total defect score =	40

A large number of different scores will be recorded using this technique. In order to simplify the categorisations we can now place these scores into a table to enable us to make sense of them.

Score range	Broad definition	Category	Detailed definition
1 to 10	Good	1	As new building condition
11 to 25	Good	2	None or only slight defects, visible symptoms of the ageing process.
26 to 55	Moderate	3	Many slight and/or some substantial defects, more than half of the component life-span has passed.
56 to 115	Moderate	4	Substantial defects, remaining life-span is limited and not difficult to predict.
116 to 235	Bad	5	Very substantial defects, the component has reached the end of its life-span and replacement or major repair is necessary.
236 +	Bad	6	The component is completely worn out, almost total performance loss. The component should have been replaced at an earlier date.

Once the defect scores have been calculated and placed within the condition scales of 1 to 6, the relative importance of the defect has been established. So for the three examples above the relative importance would be:

Defect	Defect score	Condition category
1	2000	6 (i.e. 235+) Bad
2	1	1 (i.e. 1) Good
3	40	3 (26 to 55) Moderate

Defect 1 needs urgent attention, now! Defect 2 is 'as new' and could be monitored or minor repairs undertaken. Defect 3 could be repaired as part of a planned programme unless this is an isolated incident for that group of stock.

Defect scoring can be used on all an RSL's stock or on a sample of reference properties. The scores and condition categorisation will then produce an overall picture as to the condition of the stock.

Work prioritisation

Defect scores provide a set of required maintenance activities. This is not the same as a maintenance programme, which is determined by the financial position and maintenance policy of an RSL. The total cost of required maintenance activities often exceeds available maintenance budgets, especially when a maintenance backlog exists.

Where there is a backlog, defect scoring will help to decide which activities can be cancelled or postponed, and which work is so urgent it must be completed first. This informed decision-making should lead to a position where gradually backlogs can be reduced and works of a less serious nature can be planned for the future.

Various criteria can be applied to prioritise work. For example,

1. What will be the performance decrease by postponing the activity?

Performance decrease on each of the following grounds is recorded:

▼ safety - a threat to the personal well being of residents and/or visitors

▼ health - prejudicial to the welfare of the residents and/or visitors

▼ function - the components continuing ability to function/work effectively

▼ aspect - the way a component looks

The decrease in performance is expressed on a three point scale; c = slight, b = clear and a = severe. A combination of factor and effect gives a value on a six point scale of performance decrease shown in the table below.

			Increasing priority →		
1	2	3	4	5	6
				Safety	
			C	B	A
			Health		
		C	B	A	
		Function			
	C	B	A		
	Aspect				
C	B	A			

Above: table indicates increasing priority on a six point scale.

From the table we can note that a component recorded as having a slight performance decrease on safety grounds would register a higher priority rating than a severe aesthetic/aspect performance loss. This exercise is a snapshot in time. The rate at which any specific component loses performance is subject to a great deal of variation and will depend upon a number of factors. These can be component dependent e.g. poor specification, design detailing, dependent upon environmental conditions e.g. climate, temperature, dampness, or upon biological agents e.g. mould, or as a consequence of use/misuse.

The scale can be adjusted to reflect the relative priority an RSL places on performance decrease on each of the grounds, e.g. an RSL may wish to increase its priority on tackling health risks. The scale can then be moved up to categories 4, 5 & 6 alongside the safety issues.

2. Identifying the costs of postponing specific maintenance activities.

It is helpful to categorise the costs of postponing maintenance work on an objective basis. The table below scores the risk that delay will lead to significant cost increases.

⟵ Increasing priority ⟶					
1	2	3	4	5	6
No increase of repair cost in time		Proportional increase		Exponential increase of repair costs	
Cost is stable with the passage of time		Costs increase in line with the passage of time		Costs increase at a greater rate than would be expected in line with the passage of time	

Above: an example of a cost development and implications assessment

If you assess that a specific defect falls within categories 5 and 6 then works are urgently required because time delays will result in a rapid increase in cost. For example, missing roof tiles could result in water penetration to ceilings and services with possible ceiling collapse, dangerous services, wet rot, vermin attack etc. If, however, the postponement of work to replace some fixtures and fittings which does not pose a health & safety risk would not lead to an increase in costs over time the work would fall into categories 1 and 2.

The survey work to prioritise the work will need to be broken up into manageable proportions. Based upon local knowledge, the areas of greatest maintenance concern should be tackled first.

You can experiment with defect scoring using the blank example on the computer disk with this guide.

How to use the method effectively

Once the backlog of maintenance work has been identified and programmes put in place, defect scoring can be continued to identify future programmes of work as well as evaluating the effectiveness of works already completed. Defect scoring can be used whenever a property is visited. Any serious maintenance items can be quickly identified as can any new minor problems before they become a major maintenance item. Defect scoring will quickly identify any 'health and safety' issues including those that may become the subject of litigation.

The methodology of defect scoring can only be effective if all staff using the system do so consistently. Periodic benchmarking will be necessary to ensure that all staff are continuing to interpret the scoring system in the same way.

A regular review of the 'attributes' will also be necessary to ensure that the required amount of information, relevant to local knowledge, is collected. This may mean reducing or increasing the number of attributes.

This methodology has the advantage of identifying the worst problems first. Over a period of time this should mean that the seriousness of any maintenance reduces and long-term benefits will accrue. Defect scoring encourages an objective collection of data relating to the RSL's stock. It puts those works into a priority order. It helps to assess the likely effect on the component if maintenance is postponed and the effect on forecasts of deferring maintenance work.

> **Case study**
>
> Case study 8 **Moseley and District HA: Grading component deterioration – defect scoring (see page 84)**

Defect scoring will not produce a priced maintenance plan. For this other methods must be used, to complete the exercise.

5.6 Quinquennial and regular inspections

Description

Quinquennial and regular inspections are essential to achieve a high standard of property maintenance for smaller RSLs. Quinquennial inspections must be carried out by suitably qualified surveyors and will include a detailed appraisal of the condition of the building in order to identify its repair and future maintenance requirements. The inspection will include all elements of a property's structure, services and finishes. in addition to detecting faults that need rectifying, the inspection should identify areas of work that must be carried out in order to prevent problems occurring in the future.

From this assessment, a maintenance plan is developed which can be used to develop a forecast of expenditure for the twelve months, the next five years and the longer term. A term of twenty or thirty years might be considered initially, which is sufficient to cover normally recurring maintenance items, but this must be defined according to the requirements of the RSL. The level of detail in the plan will be greater for the shorter time scales.

In addition, all buildings should be inspected at regular intervals, at least annually, to ensure that there are no developing problems and that general maintenance work is regularly carried out in accordance with a time schedule. From these regular inspections, the maintenance plan can be updated.

How to set up the method

Inspection
If you have recently had an inspection then a report on this, plus a knowledge of the work carried out since the inspection, may suffice for a forecast. If an inspection is due you will need to consider carefully how you will specify the survey.

An important factor in obtaining a successful outcome is choosing the right person to do the inspection. You should use a professionally qualified specialist who will have the necessary indemnity insurance. In cases where buildings are listed and of historic importance, the person carrying out the inspection must have had additional training to equip them to deal with the specialist nature of the work.

The recommendations contained in 'Standards of Almshouse Management', published by The Almshouse Association, form a useful guide to the process – see the References in Appendix C. This includes a pro-forma guide to commissioning which identifies the key areas that should be assessed and the form of inspection report that should be obtained. You should make sure that this report identifies the following categories of maintenance and repair work:

- very urgent work, requiring immediate attention
- urgent work not requiring immediate attention
- work that should be completed within the next five years
- likely major repairs beyond the next five years

There should also be a note of areas that need monitoring to ensure that they do not cause future problems and areas in which there is evidence that routine maintenance should be improved. In addition, you should ask for recommendations for areas of improvement in the building to make sure you comply with recent legislation, current standards, and environmental improvements.

You must ensure that the report establishes the accurate condition of the property/ies. When this is established, a 'base-line' year can be set, from which you can commence your maintenance planning.

Developing a maintenance plan
The aim of a maintenance plan is to provide a comprehensive statement of all the foreseeable maintenance needs of the property/ies, starting from the base-line year. It can then be updated annually, in the light of additional inspections carried out, to reflect the current situation and circumstances of the property/ies.

You should draw up your maintenance plan in three parts, as follows:

Part 1 - Maintenance needs that will arise during the next twelve months
In addition to maintenance work required during the next twelve months this section should include items of routine maintenance such as:

- monthly and quarterly routine inspection tests of fire and security alarms, electrical installations and fire protection systems
- half-yearly inspection of roofs and lift installations
- annual gas installation inspections
- annual clearances of gutters and downpipes
- annual inspections of drains, masonry, joinery, windows, interiors and external works
- annual inspections of service installations, clocks, fire extinguishers etc

You should also add an allowance for any unplanned items, such as broken door furniture or windows. You can make an estimate of what these items are from your experience, or your past records.

Part 2 - Likely maintenance requirements during the next five years
In addition to maintenance work required during the next five years this part should also include those items of routine maintenance described above. To this list must be added items such as five-year inspections of electrical installations, lightning protection and cyclical painting cycles. You should also allow for unplanned items, as above.

Part 3 - Likely maintenance requirement in the longer term
You will want an assessment of all longer term elements in the maintenance plan so that they are not overlooked. Items such as re-roofing, reconstruction of walls, replacement of bathroom fittings represent considerable 'one-off' requirements and should be planned for as far as possible so that adequate funding can be provided for in financial planning. In addition, you should include items of normal planned and unplanned maintenance.

The maintenance cost forecast
Once a comprehensive maintenance plan is established the development of the maintenance cost forecast is relatively straightforward. Each item of the plan has an associated cost, which will vary according to the circumstances of the RSL. In some RSLs, some of the work may be carried out by voluntary workers, but others will require the services of professionals.

These costs may be allocated to each item in the plan and then aggregated over an annual and five year time period. The use of a simple computer spreadsheet is very helpful here. It enables costs to be easily summed and accommodates changes in your plan very quickly.

In this way a simple programme for planned maintenance and repairs can be developed to cover a five year rolling period, with the first year effectively containing the forecast for the forthcoming year. The table on page 62 is an example.

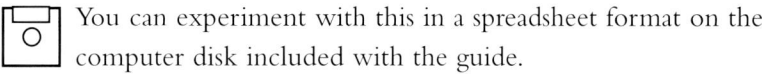 You can experiment with this in a spreadsheet format on the computer disk included with the guide.

How to maintain the method

Every year the maintenance plan must be reviewed and changes made as necessary in the light of work carried out and what has been revealed by the regular inspections. The changes introduced into the plan are then transferred into your maintenance cost forecast and this kept updated on a rolling basis. As time passes from the last quinquennial inspection, the regular inspections become more critical to ensure that no important maintenance need is missed.

Maintenance cost forecast for XXXX Association

Annual – 1999/2000 (All figures in £s) + Four-year

Maintenance item	Apr	May	Jun	Jul	Aug	Sep	Oct	Nov	Dec	Jan	Feb	Mar	00/01	01/02	02/03	03/04
Inspection Report items																
52 Arndale Road																
Replace boiler													2,400			
Re-pointing to garden wall		70					40									
Fix guard to roof outlets																
Renew fence to N boundary				450									400			
Re-point all external walls				150												
Re-fix loose bricks to rear porch area	50															
Re-surface car park area																4,500
External decoration														600	2,000	
Window replacements														4,000		
Langford House																
Replace side gate					120											
Repair tarmac to rear entrance area		346														
Combustion ventilation to boiler							145									
Install new dpc to N wall of kitchen													2,250			
External decoration						1,805										
Internal decoration to hall and stairs								210			250					
Replace bathroom fittings																
Regular inspections (all houses)																
Fire and security alarms	10	10	10	10	10	10	10	10	10	10	10	10	120	120	120	120
Electrical installation			20			20			20			20	60	60	60	60
Fire protection systems	40			40			40			40			160	160	160	160
Lifts							60						60	60	60	60
Roofs						40						40	80	80	80	80
Annual inspection								150								
Unplanned items																
Allow £50/month	50	50	50	50	50	50	50	50	50	50	50	50	600	600	600	600
Total cost	150	476	80	700	180	1,925	345	420	80	100	310	120	6,130	5,680	3,080	5,580

Page 62 Good Practice Guide: **Section B**

The log book

Each property, or group of properties, should have its own 'log book' which will contain a record of all maintenance work that has been carried out. This should be kept in the form of a diary which will record:

- any damage incurred to the building and its cause
- any removals of fittings or fixtures or changes to the building
- maintenance work carried out
- servicing work carried out
- repair work carried out
- conservation work
- alterations and extensions

Each record should contain the date work was carried out, a basic description of the work, references to the quinquennial or regular inspections that prompted the work, the firms and contractors used and the overall cost of the works including any professional fees and VAT. The entries should be cross-referenced where applicable to other documents, for example specifications or quotations.

This log book should also include the following information:

- useful particulars about the property, with photographs if appropriate
- copies of all quinquennial and regular inspections
- maintenance and service agreements,
- copies of current regulations and recommendations applicable, such as fire precautions

The book can also form a depository for items such as insurance certificates and fire alarm inspection certificates etc. The up-to-date log book becomes an invaluable resource for all who have an interest in the property. It is particularly useful when there is a change of supervision.

How to use the method effectively

Using this method of forecasting, the smaller RSL will have a clear view of its maintenance costs the next twelve months, a five year medium term plan and a long term forecast of likely maintenance expenditure.

The effective use of the method depends upon:

- a good quality quinquennial inspection. If this is not carried out to a properly defined specification, the required information will not be obtained
- the systematic implementation of regular inspections
- the annual updating of the maintenance plan to reflect the work that has been carried out during the previous year and also incorporate any new needs that have come to light from regular inspections

▼ the rolling forward of the maintenance cost forecast, to provide a current view of the forward cost commitments

▼ an accurate log book for the property/ies

The maintenance plan and cost forecast must be updated when major work is undertaken, for example to comply with new legislative requirements or in response to re-modelling of the property.

This method provides a forecast of the future maintenance costs for the RSL. It should be seen as complementary to budgetary allocation systems such as that recommended by The Almshouse Association (see References in Appendix C) whereby annual additions to the expenditure budget are set aside to provide investment funds for maintenance costs using an Extraordinary Repair Fund (the ERF), a Cyclical Maintenance Fund (the CMF) as well as routine maintenance provision. The Association provides advice to its members about what cost figures should be applied in each of these areas, categorised by properties that are new or are over 20 years old. This system enables investment provision to be made now for future costs and as such represents an example of good practice for the smaller RSL.

> **Case study**
>
> Case study 9 **Abbeyfield (Solihull): Profile of a small RSL (see page 86)**

5.7 Strengths and weaknesses of current techniques

Explanatory notes to the table on page 65

(1) This information can be remedied to an extent by the use of actual life expectancies and costs as part of a sensitivity analysis. There is a wide variation in life expectancy values even for the same building component in the same situation under the same circumstances.

(2) The lack of accurate data characteristics will present problems for a number of RSLs. Exact component specification, causes for failure, recording of incidence of non identical replacement can all impact on the accuracy of the process. Such problems can largely be overcome when combining life-cycle costing with an attribute survey.

(3) Life-cycle costing is based on component replacements and costs being undertaken on planned maintenance basis. In practice components have often passed their average life-spans and are still retained, with those that have already failed being picked up as more expensive, responsive, works.

(4) This method does not take into account repairs backlogs or the current condition of the stock. Many of the components should have been repaired at a much earlier time and initial expenditure profiles will bring most replacements activities within a short-term framework. This technique is not appropriate for discerning the extent and nature of this backlog or the current condition of the stock.

Method	Planned	Unplanned	1 Yr	1–5 Yrs	5+ Yrs	Strengths	Weaknesses
Historical costing	✓	✓	✓			• Trends in responsive and cyclical repairs costs can be projected over the short term • Quick and inexpensive method	• Unsuitable for long term projections • Indicates what has been spent before and not what maintenance work is required • accuracy depends on level of detail recorded on earlier maintenance costs
Zero-based budgeting	✓	✓	✓			• Forces re-examination of priorities and justification for all activities • Good discipline • Useful to target activities to improve effectiveness	• Time-consuming to implement if real benefits are to be obtained • Can become cumbersome if not controlled
Life-cycle costing	✓				✓	• A good forecasting tool when totalled over a number of properties and taken over a period • Component life-spans are available from a variety of sources • Local variations in life-spans costs can be incorporated using a sensitivity analysis • When linked into condition surveys this approach can result in the formulation of repair programmes	• Wide variations in component life-spans (1) • Wide variations in component replacement costs (2) • Lack of datacharacteristics • There is an assumption that all replacement works occur in a planned way (3) • This method does not take account of the condition of stock or backlogs in repairs (4)
Attribute surveys	✓			✓	✓	• Assessments based on actual condition of stock in 1-5 year time band • Benefits associated with surveys in general can be applied • Strengths as life-cycle costing	• Sample needs to be representative or extrapolations will be inaccurate • Key pitfalls associated with surveys in general are identified in Section A. • Weaknesses as life-cycle costing
Defect scoring	✓		✓	✓		• Assessments based on actual condition of stock • Repair programmes can be costed and generated to undertake replacements as they are needed • The method accepts that work required may be in excess of available resources and offers guidance for the prioritisation of programmes	• Staff need to be well trained in this standardised grading system • This pro-active task of repair/ replacement data gathering may generate extra works orders in itself • Key pitfalls associated with surveys in general identified in Section A
Quin-quennial and regular inspections	✓		✓	✓	✓	• Detailed appraisals and maintenance projections based on actual condition of stock • Ongoing record of maintenance works carried out on each unit, results of inspections and certificates registered in 'log books'	• Inspections must be carried out by a suitably qualified person • Accuracy of anticipating elemental / component failure over 3 years may have a significant margin of error

Appendix A
Summary of Action Points

Section A
Developing and implementing strategies for maintenance cost forecasting

Stage 1
Developing a strategy for maintenance cost forecasting

Making sure the strategy integrates with the organisation's Business Plan

> ☞ **Action Point**
>
> You will need to make sure that the work you are going to do on maintenance cost forecasting is properly integrated into your organisation's existing business planning system. This will need agreement from the senior management team and ultimately from the Board. They will need to understand how this important cyclical process works.

Linking asset management and reinvestment strategies to maintenance cost forecasting

> ☞ **Action Point**
>
> You will need to make sure that the work you are doing on maintenance cost forecasting links to any existing strategies on asset management and reinvestment.

Identifying who should be involved in the development of forecasts

> ☞ **Action Point**
>
> You will need to seek agreement to adopting a bottom up approach to maintenance cost forecasting which involves both maintenance and finance staff in developing and reviewing the forecasts.

Defining terms

> ☞ **Action Points**
>
> 1) You will need to agree the terminology and definitions used within your RSL. This will involve discussions with finance, development and housing management staff.
>
> 2) Once the terminology and definitions have been agreed you will need to ensure that your manual and IT systems reflect the changes. This is likely to include reviewing coding systems for maintenance expenditure and scheme appraisal systems. You will need to do your own careful check to ensure that changes are worked through all the organisation's systems.

The effect of improvements

> ☞ **Action Point**
>
> You will need to ensure that your forecasting system includes an improvement review mechanism particularly for short and medium term forecasts.

Finding out about stock condition

> ☞ **Action Points**
>
> If you are planning to do a stock condition survey for the first time or you want to review the way you currently do them, you should:
>
> 1) Read up on the subject using the References in Appendix C in this guide as a starting point.
>
> 2) Speak to colleagues in other RSLs about their experiences and learn from them.
>
> 3) Ensure you give sufficient time to planning the survey before you start to do it. It will save you time, money and grief if you do.
>
> 4) Make sure the planning team is led by someone with maintenance expertise but includes people with IT skills as well.

Establishing the time scales for forecasts

> ☞ **Action Point**
>
> You will need to agree the time scales you wish to adopt for forecasting at senior management team and Board level.

Stage 2
Implementing the maintenance cost forecasting strategy

Building flexibility into forecasting

> ☞ **Action Point**
>
> You will need to set up a system to review and revise long, medium and short term forecasts to ensure that they reflect changing external factors and up-to-date knowledge of stock condition.

Checking and fine-tuning forecasts

> ☞ **Action Points**
>
> 1) You will need to set up a property database and a system to keep it up to date. To do this effectively you will need to work with your RSL's IT expert and the development team. They will have a key role to play in providing information about new schemes.
>
> 2) You will need to ensure that your forecasting review process builds in the use of out-turn results so that your forecasts become more personalised to the RSL's own circumstances over time.

Prioritising planned maintenance work

> ☞ **Action Point**
>
> You will need to agree a system for prioritising planned maintenance programmes at senior management team and Board level.

Deciding how you will procure maintenance work

> ☞ **Action Point**
>
> You will need to review your current methods of procurement and assess the impact of the methods you choose on your short and medium term forecasts. You will need to get agreement at senior management and Board level to changes in procurement strategy.

Stage 3
Linking the work you do on maintenance cost forecasting to other current issues for RSLs.

The Housing Corporation's performance standards

> ☞ **Action Point**
>
> You will need to develop a clear statement of what standard of maintenance your RSL believes will achieve this 'reasonable and lettable condition'. Arriving at this definition will involve discussion with applicants, residents and housing management staff to agree what is necessary and affordable. This standard will need to be agreed at senior management and Board level.

> ☞ **Action Point**
>
> Rents are a major source of income to fund future maintenance work. These restrictions on rent increases will affect your RSL's ability to fund future programmes. You will need to assess the impact of this change on your forecasts. If the rent increase restrictions affect your organisation's ability to meet essential future maintenance commitments you will need to alert the senior management team and the Board. Your RSL may then wish to raise this issue with the Corporation.

> ☞ **Action Points**
>
> 1) Maintenance cost forecasting is part of your maintenance policy and procedure. You will need to provide residents with information about how you do it.
>
> 2) You will need to involve residents appropriately in the long, medium and short term planning process for maintenance.
>
> 3) You will need to ensure that risks associated with maintenance cost forecasting are included in the risk management exercise.

Best Value

> ☞ **Action Points**
>
> 1) You will need to keep up-to-date with Best Value as it develops nationally and make sure you are aware of how your RSL is developing and implementing Best Value internally.
>
> 2) If you are seeking out best practice on maintenance cost forecasting, using it to improve the way you forecast maintenance costs and you are involving residents in the process, you are already demonstrating Best Value techniques.

Energy efficiency

> ☞ **Action Points**
>
> 1) You will need to incorporate any agreed energy efficiency targets in your forecasts
>
> 2) You will need to ensure that the results of energy efficiency audits are used to inform the forecasts you prepare.

Information technology (IT)

> ☞ **Action Points**
>
> You will need to:
>
> 1) Invest some time in getting to grips with IT so that you can contribute effectively to organisational discussions. This applies whatever the size of your RSL.
>
> 2) Analyse your needs thoroughly before you invest in a system.
>
> 3) Allow plenty of time to discuss requirements and agree a specification - however long it is, it is unlikely to be wasted.
>
> 4) Allow for future change. do not think that today's answer will hold firm for ever.
>
> 5) Be clear about what data you wish to hold, what data is fixed and what data will change. Remember that your existing data, in whatever form, is valuable.

Appendix B
Case studies

1 Case study 1   **The introduction of an asset management strategy (see p.70)**
Touchstone HA

2 Case study 2   **The difficulties in realising the full benefits of an active planned programme (see p.72)**
Collingwood HA Ltd

3 Case study 3   **Rolling stock condition surveys (see p.73)**
Hexagon HA

4 Case study 4   **Periodic stock condition surveys (see p.76)**
Downland Housing Group Ltd

5 Case study 5   **Historical cost forecasting (see p.78)**
Marches HA Ltd

6 Case study 6   **Life cycle costing as part of an integrated property management system (see p.80)**
Threshold Tennant Trust

7 Case study 7   **Attribute surveys (see p.81)**
Salford Community HA

8 Case study 8   **Grading component deterioration - defect scoring (see p.84)**
Moseley and District Churches HA Ltd

9 Case study 9   **Profile of a small RSL (see p.86)**
The Abbeyfield (Solihull) Society Ltd

Case study 1
The introduction of an asset management strategy

Touchstone HA manages 12,000 units across the Midlands. In an attempt to manage the maintenance of existing stock effectively, Touchstone is adopting an asset management strategy. Touchstone has worked to establish investment criteria to secure the long term future of their assets and the rental stream they produce. This case study examines the way the stock appraisal system links into the wider asset management system.

A draft discussion paper on asset management was presented to the Executive Board early in 1997 outlining the current and future options for the RSL and covering:

1 Effective asset management

Core questions on the relative priority and links that are required between the life-cycle of the stock, day-to-day repairs, cyclical inspections, the views of tenants and of local housing management in the formulation of a planned maintenance and refurbishment programme were raised and discussed in some detail.

2 The strategy for initiating a planned maintenance programme, including:

- knowledge of stock based on a stock condition survey, re-surveyed on a routine basis and linked to an accurate record of the condition of individual properties
- the establishment of a specific standard to which the association is aiming to maintain all its stock
- a rolling stock renewal plan which is costed, prioritised and moves toward the target of 60-70% spending on planned, as against reactive, repairs

3 A progressive strategy

The need for the stock renewal plan to be informed by a better understanding of the existing stock condition, stock condition trends and all the factors that influence investment decisions.

4 Stock condition survey

An essential component of any asset management system is good quality accurate information on the condition of the stock. Touchstone HA has implemented an inspection programme of 20% of the stock per year. Voids are surveyed as they occur. The stock condition survey was designed in-house with help from external consultants. The consultants also carried out a quality control audit on a percentage of the completed surveys. The data is held in an ACCESS database on a networked personal computer. The personal computer holds Touchstone's life-cycle model, giving information on the predicted need to spend. Links between this and the database have been developed by IT consultants.

5 Survey resources

Maintenance surveyors have recently significantly changed in their work responsibilities with the introduction of an on-line maintenance management system operated from a call centre. This is taking much of the workload associated with voids and responsive repairs away from the surveyors. The new role of surveyors at Touchstone is primarily concerned with covering the 'cradle to the grave' whole-life maintenance of all properties in management.

The Asset Management Information System (AMIS)

Touchstone are building a prototype AMIS linking their AS400 database and networked PCs. The prototype uses a management information system as the user interface to map information into:

- geographical information systems: such systems will be able to assess groups of properties, carry out analysis by area, type of property, voids and those requiring re-improvement, in addition to identifying 'hotspots' in voids and maintenance costs
- EXCEL: used for spreadsheet analysis, projections and graphs
- SPSSX: a statistical tool which can produce detailed statistical projections

There are four components to the AMIS:

1 Physical assessment
This involves a thorough examination of the previous 5 to 10 years of historical information on reactive, voids and planned maintenance. These are projected forward for each of the categories over 1–5 years at today's prices. Information on property plans/deconversions and photographs will be available for persons interested in drilling behind the total forecast figures.

2 Financial assessment
Assessments are made into likely income generation based on historical knowledge. A series of assumptions can be put into the system on voids/bad debts, tenancy occupancy periods, arrears figures by income band/type of property/area etc., to gauge rental stream as a result of taking a particular course of action.

3 Environmental assessment
A whole range of issues affecting the environment in which Touchstone's stock is located are examined. Areas include: looking at housing need assessments (what the demand is for the units from waiting list/transfers, demand from the LA etc), what's happening around the units, tenure patterns, population patterns, local and regional regeneration works. Information on local rents and affordability issues will be important factors in assessing the environment.

4 Option appraisal
A 'do nothing' baseline, generated from the data, is taken by the system for all properties and a figure for income and expenditure is derived. Queries can request financial forecasts at net-present-values and for a range of options. Certain options will make more financial sense but may not be as politically palatable or in tune with housing needs/tenant survey feedback.

Touchstone HA are pleased with the progress to date on AMIS. The integration of stock condition information, life-cycle model data, option appraisal, environmental and tenants' perspectives into the process from the start are all good indicators for the successful operation of this strategic approach.

Case study 2

The difficulties in realising the full benefits of an active planned programme

Collingwood Housing Association has approximately 5,000 units in Manchester, Salford, Liverpool and surrounding areas. Collingwood has increased its planned works expenditure over the last 5 years in order to make cost efficiencies in batching, commissioning and procuring works and to further improve on tenant satisfaction levels.

This RSL has closely examined maintenance cost information for all categories of maintenance from 1993 to 1998. Over this period the effects of pursuing a large planned programme on the number and cost of responsive repairs orders were scrutinised, to establish if reactive work had diminished in light of the increase in planned maintenance.

Fig. 1 (below) compares planned (including cyclical) and reactive expenditure over the 6 year period.

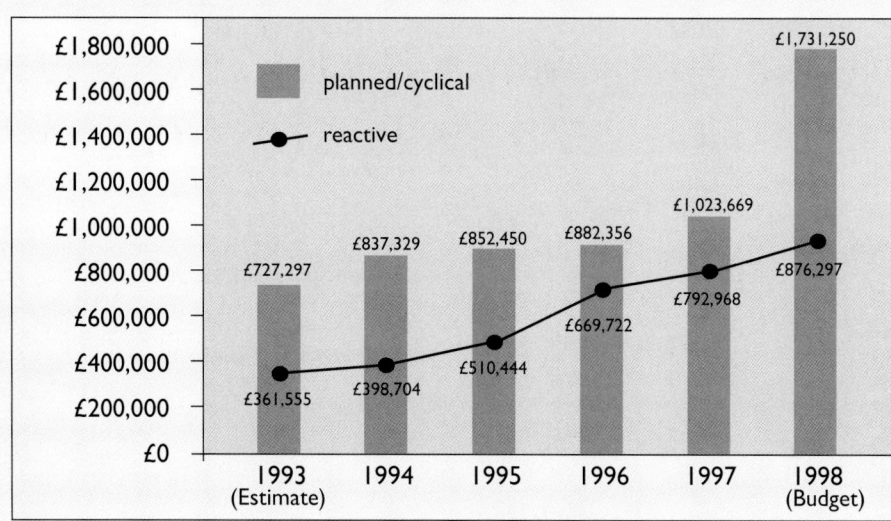

Above: comparison of planned and reactive expenditure over a 6-year period

Collingwood also examined particular refurbishment programmes and reviewed the subsequent impact on responsive repairs. In Fig 2 (below) five schemes are analysed for the number of repairs orders and costs before and after kitchen refurbishments were carried out in 1995. Although there is a reduction in the number and cost of repairs following refurbishment works, it is not significant. The value of each repairs order appears also to have reduced post works. Some works which should have been picked up under defects liability may have been processed as repairs.

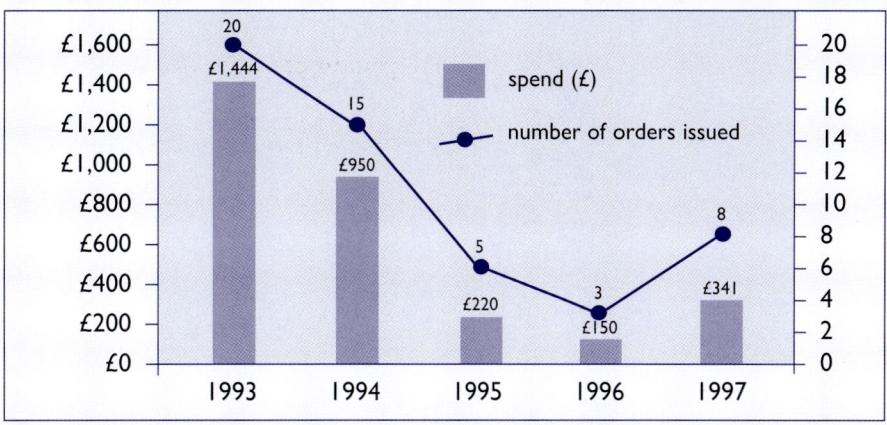

Above: analysis of kitchen repairs over a 5-year period (refurbishment of 5 schemes carried out in 1995)

Collingwood are clear that there are serious difficulties in analysing effectively the cost savings created by planned maintenance. Even on a single scheme basis, such as above, factors such as unpredictablity of repair reporting by tenants, changes in stock size, stock ageing, etc. make comparisons very difficult. When considering the whole stock it is even more so. Cost savings are often spurious. Cost benefits associated with some works such as thermal insulation may be directed to the tenant and not the association. Double glazing replacements save on cyclical costs, however frame cleaning and more expensive repairs reduce such a saving.

It is clear that kitchen refurbishments, double glazing and thermal insulation works lead to increased tenant satisfaction. Tenants benefit from the reduction in unpredictable repairs which arise as a direct consequence of increased planned programmes.

Collingwood are committed to continue with its policies on planned maintenance because:

▼ of cost savings to tenants and the association

▼ it gives greater tenant satisfaction

▼ it demonstrates a professional approach to maintenance

▼ it is a positive approach to asset management and reinvestment in the stock portfolio

Case study 3
Rolling stock condition surveys

Hexagon HA has over 2,100 general needs homes and over 300 supported housing and nursing home bedspaces in south east London covering Lewisham, Southwark, Greenwich and surrounding boroughs. The stock is approximately 80% rehab. and 20% new build. Routine maintenance accounts for 29% of rent spent by the association in 1996/1997. In addition 19% is put towards stock improvements and 4% towards voids and bad debts.

Hexagon HA operate a structured system of retrieving stock condition information through the use of their existing improvement, cyclical and day-to-day repair activities. The objective of this case study is to examine how cyclical and day-to-day repair activities can be extended to cover the structured recording of overall stock condition.

Hexagon had a large scale 'snapshot' stock condition survey (SCS) carried out in 1993/1994 covering 92% (difficulties in access prevented an even greater coverage) of the general needs stock. This SCS was carried out in-house using temporary staff. The work on establishing the database and loading information onto the database was carried out externally. The clear intention behind the SCS was to generate the information which would allow the association to bring up all the existing stock to an acceptable standard.

The SCS pro-formas were kept relatively basic, covering key components, and targeted at producing the necessary data to identify units that would require attention to bring them into good order.

Rolling stock condition sheets were compiled from the following four sources:

1 Records updated following large SCS
Replacements and renewals of key components identified following the initial survey were entered into the database at the time of works.

2 Voids
A stock condition survey sheet/printout is being used by void surveyors for all inspections. The printout will confirm the previous condition and prompt the surveyor to update the record. Where no previous information exists a new SCS sheet will be completed.

3 Stock improvement team
As a result of the large SCS, a programme of improvement works was initiated by Hexagon HA to redress the quality of some of the poorest of its stock. The surveyors on this team also have responsibility for carrying out survey updates on units that are on the programme or may be considered for the programme.

4 Cyclical
A rolling 20% per year programme is undertaken. Attempts are made by all surveyors to access the units to complete fully the SCS sheets and the external surveys are updated. Slow turnover voids, which have not been surveyed, will be picked up manually for an urgent inspection. Within the current IT upgrades being considered at Hexagon HA is a 'flagging' system on the property database which will pinpoint such 'omitted' units far more readily for all surveyors.

Resources for rolling SCS

SCS updating is made a part of all surveyors duties, on a weekly basis. Issues around better access to the information held will make this mandatory task less time consuming and expensive. The IT review will address this issue. There is a commitment to undertaking the rolling stock condition survey programme by void, cyclical and stock improvement surveyors. The information gathered is of good quality and is invaluable in the formulation of repair programmes in outline and anticipating future maintenance costs.

On average, surveyors spend 20% of their working week carrying out the surveys. Following the snapshot in 1993/1994 the stock improvement team, whose role is largely to write specifications, project manage and administer the contracts, were in a position to identify programmes of work quickly, which in turn enabled them to draw in significant amounts of Major Repairs Housing Association Grant into their programmes.

Once surveyors have completed the sheets they are input onto the SCS register. At present the information is held on a networked PC. Integration, or re-inputting all information on the central database, are issues that will be resolved during the current IT review. Information already on the PC and from recently completed SCS sheets are assessed and analysed whenever specific planned programmes are being considered.

Hexagon has roofing, central heating and general electrical planned programmes which feed off the information from the rolling inspection programme. Furthermore, if two or more elements in a unit are graded as poor, the case is referred through to the stock improvement/package improvement to voids programme (which can include major repairs, deconversions, sound insulation etc.).

Difficulties for Hexagon are mainly concerned with IT. The information from the snapshot and the ongoing rolling inspections appears very robust with a high level of commitment from surveyors and staff members to its success. The IT problem is two-fold; firstly the system is not on the (CONTEXT) database and cannot be accessed easily by surveyors who require information on the units; and secondly the initial input and updating on the networked PC requires a considerable amount of effort and, again, problems of accessibility to the information make the task one that requires considerable use of scarce staff time. The feasibility of SCS data storage through the use of CONTEXT's planned and cyclical module is currently being explored.

Other problems have included access to the properties. A significant number of units remain uninspected from the inside, despite numerous attempts to establish suitable times for the inspections to be carried out. This has caused some difficulties in assessing the condition of properties and programming repair works.

This method of carrying out a SCS is ideal for Hexagon HA with its diversely spread street properties. A snapshot survey on a high % of the stock would be very expensive and would not meet the association's desire to continually, year on year, glean information for their repair/stock improvement programmes and future maintenance cost forecasts.

Hexagon has found that:

▼ a structured process of inspections has been carried out without significant slippage

▼ information sheets double as printouts of the original survey and deterioration can be checked

▼ it can filter information into repair programmes

▼ it has been able to focus on the specific requirements of the IT review covering all areas concerned with the rolling SCS, i.e. updating, actioning works, retrieving information and running reports on the surveys.

Case study 4
Periodic stock condition surveys

Downland Housing Group (DHG) was formed on 1st April 1996 and is the parent organisation for Downland Housing Society, Mid-Sussex Housing Association, Downland Retirement Homes, Downland Property Management Limited and Southdown Housing Association. DHG owns and manages some 12,000 homes across ten counties in the South and South East.

The first stock condition survey (SCS) was carried out in 1989 to comply with the requirements of the Housing Corporation. This initial survey had provision for updating; the software was a bespoke system by a local consultant. With hindsight this initial SCS collected too much information and was too complicated. It did however enable the Group to compile a 30-year programme.

DHG has had difficulty in identifying a suitable software solution that matches its requirements, together with the requirements that any new programme should be backward compatible to allow the transfer of existing data.

The Group's corporate development plan has identified strategic objectives for stock condition and maintenance. The aims are to provide an effective maintenance service, responding to repairs within published response times and to use a proportion of income to improve the condition of the stock. The aims are also to review the standards to be achieved for all major components, review the stock condition every five years, review maintenance and improvement priorities, set targets for maintenance and improvements to agreed standards and to achieve high quality with low ongoing maintenance costs.

In 1998 the Group commissioned a new SCS using a two stage tendering processes. Three consultants were asked to tender at Stage 1 with the winning consultant going forward to Stage 2.

Extensive consultations have been carried out with other parts of the organisation (housing management, development) as it is intended that other parts of the organisation will have access to the information system, operating something like a help-desk where a tenant can telephone to make a query and all queries will be dealt with by one telephone call. Access to data would be to view only.

Having examined 'in-house' planned maintenance modules in practice at other housing associations they were considered inappropriate for the Group's requirements. Therefore a decision was made to stay with a bespoke system provided by the successful consultant.

The SCS will be utilised to produce a strategic plan using a limited number of attributes. Costs are obtained by combining the RSL's knowledge with that of the local consultant carrying out the SCS. Costs are replacement costs.

Downlands IT department has been involved in the decision making process to ensure that the software systems and data can be integrated into a local area network.

It is envisaged that an SCS with 100% external and 10% internal will be adequate. There will be random checks carried out by in-house surveyors. Before the full SCS is implemented it is intended to carry out a pilot survey to ensure that the system, data and specification works.

Ensuring consistency is a major aim of the process, This has also involved the development section in the consultation process with the external consultant who is carrying out the SCS. The SCS will also take the opportunity to include SAP ratings and from this a programme of energy saving can be developed.

Simplicity has been the watchword in the specification of the latest SCS. Basic questions were asked such as 'what information do we want?' (avoiding unnecessary data). It was also made clear that the SCS would not be the panacea, but that it formed an important tool in the process for planned maintenance. The SCS would establish the major works programme. This would involve housing management who in turn would bring tenants into the surveying process. Tenants' wishes and fears (security is a major issue) would be filtered through in the process. If too much work is identified in any one year, then the work will be re-prioritised.

It will be the responsibility of DHG technical services to ensure that the system is updated as and when work is carried out. The SCS will also include a photograph of each property.

After the consultation period is complete, the total costs will be estimated. The resulting programme will be assessed by the finance department regarding budget implications and presented to the Board for approval.

Following this, the Group will decide what can be done in-house and what work will be placed with consultants.

In brief:

All parts of the RSL have been involved in the SCS and maintenance planning process. Previous experience of a less than perfect SCS has informed the RSL how to specify successfully the SCS the second time around.

Case study 5
Historical cost forecasting

Marches HA Ltd was created in 1994 following a Large Scale Voluntary Transfer (LSVT) of 1,850 properties from Leominster District Council. The survey undertaken at that time for the council indicated a projected spend over a 25 year period of £4.5 m for maintenance and improvements. It was subsequently realised that this covered a sample of only 15-25% of stock types and produced a very optimistic spend. The original survey concentrated on major components such as kitchens, windows and central heating.

The Technical Services Manager at Marches is responsible for producing maintenance reports for the Director of Property Services. The finance department generates all statistics and returns, business plans and budgets in conjunction with heads of departments.

There is no set technique for historical cost forecasting, however the majority of RSLs use averages of previous years' responsive/cyclical costs and project these with an uplift for inflation and possibly an allowance for ageing.

Marches HA has approached this area of work systematically with a close examination of responsive trends. In particular it analysed repair information, including costs on a systematic, month by month basis, to help in forecasting.

A series of typical responsive historical maintenance records for recent years are shown below:

Key
Number of day repair orders throughout the year

—✕— 1995/96
—○— 1996/97
—●— 1997/98
—■— 1998/99

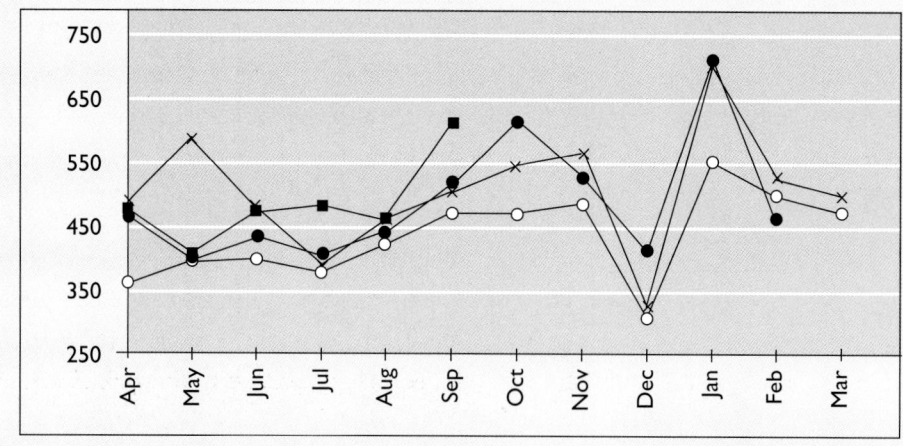

Key
Cumulative numbers of day repair orders throughout the year

—✗— 1995/96
—○— 1996/97
—●— 1997/98
—□— 1998/99

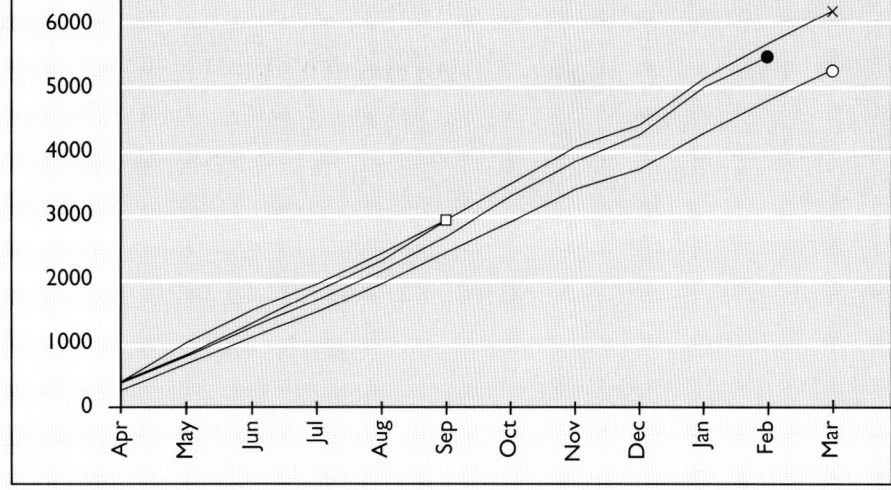

Key
Cumulative costs of day repair orders throughout the year (£ 000s)

—✗— 1995/96
—○— 1996/97
—●— 1997/98
—□— 1998/99

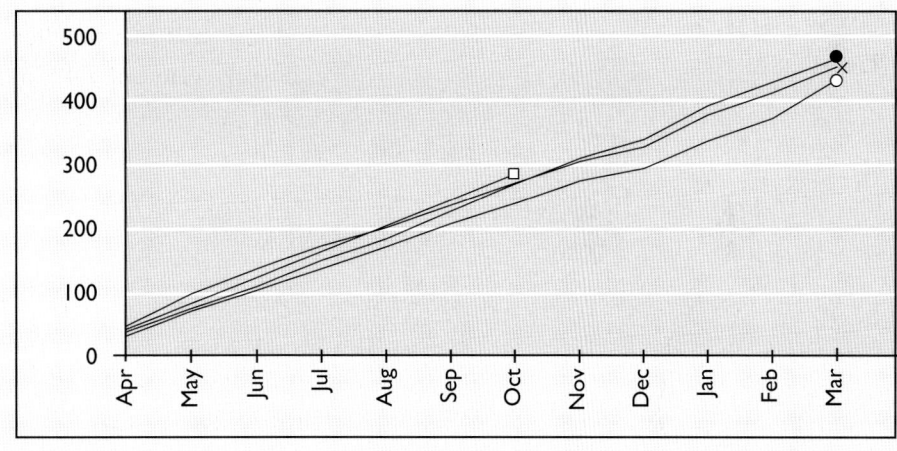

Reactive maintenance is tendered by Marches using the National Schedule of Rates (NSR) on a three year basis that may be negotiated (assessed at 16% below present cost). Although data is held on their EXCELSIS package it is analysed by transferring it into MS EXCEL to create management reports that show trends and problems. Analyses are being carried out at present to establish trends in work types, budget control and setting, Direct Labour Organisation (DLO) feasibility and identification of bad properties. Responsive repairs forecasting is generally based on a review of these recent trend projections with the addition of inflation – usually applied by the finance department. An offshoot of these maintenance trend examinations has led the association to consider the introduction of a DLO to allow technical officers to concentrate on quality rather than cost management, as at present, repair contractors tend to be QS driven. Detailed analysis is currently difficult because orders are not always placed by the codes for tasks in the NSR. However, contractor analysis is possible.

The association is keen to address the problems within IT which derive from lack of integration between various software packages. Generally, Marches feel that solutions are heading in the right direction but that reports are still based on going back to first principles. Further work is needed before standard reports using trend analysis are generated in an integrated manner.

Case study 6
Life-cycle costing as part of an integrated property management system

Threshold Tennant Trust (TTT) has some 4,000 units, having grown from 650 units ten years ago. TTT has from the late 1980's adopted a planned approach to property management with a view to achieving high quality standards based on a corporate reinvestment strategy. TTT's view is that property management systems, incorporating an integrated life-cycle model, together with a carefully specified process, can overcome problems and difficulties in co-ordinating a multi-departmental approach.

TTT have had a computer based stock survey system for some time; this is continually being improved and extended as a customised system. The philosophy behind the IT development has been the need for a flexible system of information and planning tools which can change as expectations and requirements change.

TTT are striving to achieve:

▼ an enhanced level of customer satisfaction with their repair service

▼ financial resources and organisational systems in place to maintain good lettable standards over the whole life-time of the property

▼ bench marked standards of amenity

▼ continuous improvement, particularly in the areas of sound proofing and energy conservation.

TTT recognise that property management is a multifaceted activity where finance and development have an input and equally finance and development should have access to the outputs of the maintenance function. Property services managers will provide outputs for long term planning of the stock. The Trust uses its collective experience of life-cycles to alter those cycles particularly where they are affected by the tenant group. Their customised system allows the usual manipulation of the LCC spreadsheet but also benefits from a responsive 'flagging' mechanism which ensures co-ordination between planned and responsive on repair or replacement activities for all pre-identified elements.

TTT's corporate objectives recognise the multidisciplinary aspect of property management including technical, financial and customer services. This has led to a methodology for an integrated and dynamic approach. The framework adopted includes systems and procedures such as; a database computer system used to store and manipulate data and to provide the output for financial, maintenance, property management and customer service aspects; data gathering and up-dating of information (initially this was a stock condition survey (SCS) followed by input on new stock); additional surveys and updates following repair and improvement programmes.

TTT recognises that systems which are not integrated can become out-of-date very quickly. The data gathering included an extensive programme of photographs, including major aspects of each individual property which may have maintenance implications in the future. The SCS gathered 31 attributes, mostly external. Financial analyses, current assessments and future predictions are to be based on the total stock at any one time not simply on the surveyed stock. Costings and year by year predictions are kept in current day terms utilising schedules of rates and current experience. The system's financial analysis includes future cost projections of all planned maintenance, major repairs and improvements, the calculation of sinking funds, leaseholder liabilities, total income to maintenance and loan funding needs.

The dynamic financial model predicts total costs and income to achieve the corporate goal of effective long term planning for property management. The system provides the information needed by departments to fulfil their functions. The information service includes such things as SAP ratings, carbon-dioxide emissions, insurance re-building values, global financial modelling and as-built information.

TTT's view is that poor information systems are time wasting and frustrating. Increasingly staff and customers expect to see easy to use and intuitive information retrieval systems. the internal network is being extended as more staff see the benefits of the IT system. The visual details held on properties communicates information very effectively. The type of information generally available for trust wide general inquiries includes property attributes, amenities for letting purposes, planned repair programmes due in the future, non-confidential financial information, photographs, plans and the facility to hold operating instructions for installations such as central heating controls.

From the SCS, data held in the system allows automatically produced specifications and drawings to be packaged for use in either serial or traditional tendering procurement programmes. A common system of coding attributes provides the link from the database to the works programme. This dynamic link also allows the up-dating of the database following the completion of the works. Any alterations to plans and/or updates to photographs are filtered into the system.

The implementation of IT throughout the Trust has created cultural changes, but the whole Trust is now integrated into the decision making process.

Case study 7
Attribute surveys

Salford Community Housing Association (SCHA) was established in 1975 and has 2,000 units in management in Salford, Manchester, Blackburn and surrounding areas. This RSL is, like many associations, faced with an increasingly ageing stock and the pressing need to establish costed plans for the future maintenance and improvement of its housing. Maintenance works expenditure averaged £670 per property in 1995, with the association spending over £1,179,000 on repairs and maintenance in that year. This amount was split between £879,000 for day-to-day and £300,000 for major repairs and improvements. Eighteen percent of all work undertaken by SCHA is by private contractors.

SCHA commissioned a large scale stock condition survey (SCS) in 1993 (100% rehab. and 30% of new build). The statement on stock condition was generally encouraging and SCHA were also fortunate to receive a significant injection of Major Repairs Social Housing Grant to assist in repairing some of the worst units. However, the survey brief although producing a mass of information, especially on backlog repairs, was not sufficiently tight to enable costed future maintenance plans to be generated. This area became the focus of the current attribute survey and 'repair profiling' exercise.

SCHA were keen to initiate a 5 yearly attribute survey programme which would create repair profiles in order to assess dwelling performance and to forecast the costs of future repairs.

Consideration within the carefully drafted brief was given to:-

- specific aims and objectives of the survey
- proposed uses of the survey
- the final outcomes of the survey
- the scope
- the level of detail
- the method of the survey
- environmental impact/energy audit
- how the results were to be used
- the implementation of a thoroughly tested user friendly IT output.

SCHA undertook a structured approach in pursuing an attribute survey. In the first instance consultants were invited to tender for the brief and a series of interviews were held to discuss specific proposals in more detail. An area of particular importance was the measures that each consultant would put in place, if successful, to ensure consistency from their team of surveyors.

The successful consultancy offered a small dedicated team of surveyors (ARICS/MCIOB qualified) with an experienced project manager overseeing a range of checks and balances on the quality of work and consistency in inspections and in getting interim and final reports in on time. The structure and form of the 'repair profiles' was largely informed by the NHF publication 'Stock Condition Surveys: A basic guide for housing associations' (1994).

Elements and sub-elements were broken down into 44 repair items. Psion 'Workabout' hand held data capture systems (using Data Build Power Survey software) were used and pre-set costs were adopted. Component identification was obtained from historical and development records as well as improvement programme information. The task of determining the age of useful life of the repair items were made easier by the 5 year banding that formed part of the profile. More detailed information was recorded for failure within 5 years in order to feed into the repair programme. The lifespans decided for components were, in practice, BRE figures adjusted with local knowledge.

SCHA chose to adopt a full attribute survey on all rehabs and a percentage of new build to create their repair profiles. Instead of creating certain property types for the profiles, particular units or scheme profiles were assessed through IT manipulation of the database response and query functions.

The problems of the past stock condition survey have assisted greatly in the focusing of the current works. There are likely to be some discrepancies with life-cycles as this is an area where SCHA does not have a significant amount of historical data. However, this in time will improve as actual out-turns are used for future projections.

Good information and consultation with all interested parties about the SCS process has eased potential misunderstandings concerning the purpose of the inspection programme (ie tenants wondering what is going on with their day-to-day repairs after the 'inspection'). SCHA are aware that IT hardware resources may need to be looked at again in view of the limited availability of PC stations able to access the final reports.

The association is determined to see the attribute information in an easily updateable form and has made provisions for another survey to be undertaken again in 5 years time.

SCHA feels that the success of the exercise to create repair profiles from an attribute survey and the other aims clearly expressed within the consultants brief will be met, because of the focused nature of the brief. Lessons learnt from the initial stock condition exercise were applied in this subsequent attribute condition survey. If the results of the survey succeed in accurately informing the planned programme process for SCHA then the exercise will have been well worthwhile.

Whilst carrying out this exercise SCHA has found it vital to:

- spend a good deal of time and effort on the brief
- be focused on the aims and objectives
- create strict deadlines for progress and interim reports and survey completion
- make adequate financial allowances for further periodic snapshot surveys to update records.

Case study 8
Grading component deterioration - defect scoring

Moseley & District Churches HA Ltd. manages a total of 1,400 homes in Birmingham, of which almost half are one bedroom flats or bedsits. Moseley & District has a good track record in maintenance, with 99% of all responsive jobs being completed on time - including 100% of all emergency tasks within time.

The need to establish an effective planned programme - picking up works as they largely become necessary - has led to Moseley & District undertaking a series of inspections plotting the deterioration of each unit's key elements and components. It has adopted a structured inspection programme grading or 'defect scoring' of the deterioration of elements/components within the stock. This process provides important information about short and medium term maintenance costs and allows the 'batching' of works, where possible, to enable economies of scale. Moseley & District is using life-cycle costing analysis and standardised site inspections to help to assess future disrepair and ensure there is adequate financial provision to maintain the stock in good condition.

Working on the basis that life-cycle costing analysis is based on the ideal scenario, which omits factors such as quality of installation, relationship to linked components, use or misuse, environmental factors, current maintenance policy etc., the association has elected to run a component grading inspection programme together with its desktop life-cycle analysis.

Standard life-spans are amended to reflect the association's experience and then recorded for long term forecasting purposes. Surveyors undertaking void, day-to-day (including 10-20% post inspections) and cyclical inspections are expected to complete a house condition survey sheet detailing 10 elements. The 10 elements are fencing, pitched roof, external structure, window frames, doors, bathroom fittings, kitchen fittings, electricity supply, gas supply and heating appliances. They are asked to grade deterioration for each element over a number of pre-recorded time-bands. The time-bands vary from 1–50 years depending on the life-cycles of the elements. Alterations are incorporated into the life-cycle analysis as a result of the site inspections.

Moseley & District use the EXCELSIS system at present. With this system, once the property reference number is input, it is possible to move into three life-cycle databases giving the years of replacement for particular elements. New build properties are set up on the system lifespans (averaged) are set on the database from their handover dates.

Information held on the elements makes little reference to manufacturer's make/model specifications when determining life spans; this is to keep the process straightforward. The association is of the view that with the significant deviation in all life-spans it would be wasteful of time, effort and money to create an elaborate life-cycle model for estimating long term maintenance costs. Average replacement costs for each element are entered within the database to generate a cost expenditure profile for specific years and for specific replacement activities. These life-cycle costings are adjusted through a series of standardised site inspections and the new life-span dates are entered into the database.

Works required on kitchens, bathrooms and heating are undertaken through planned programmes, whereas the others are picked up by cyclical or major repair/re-improvement programmes.

Imminent planned programmes are assessed to take into account the relative performance of replacements, current expectations and life-styles and in making improvements in energy efficiency ratings.

Planned works are tendered in stages throughout the year in order to give opportunities for smaller firms to secure contracts and as a means of monitoring the budget situation over the year.

Moseley & District is aware of some areas in which inspection programmes are in need of improvement by:

- examining the issue of updating in more detail. A review of the whole process, from ensuring the forms are taken out, completed forms are returned, input and subsequently updated are tasks that have been identified as still requiring a more rigorous approach. IT will assist in this work greatly.

- verification of data. It is often the case that major elemental replacements will occur and include other replacements where it is cost effective even if they are not yet at the end of their lives ie roofing will be done with guttering, even if the guttering is satisfactory. A process of verifying data is being considered on a cyclical basis.

The association is looking to review its IT systems and it is anticipated that the future system will assist with updates via established links between databases. The issue of subjectivity is being addressed in order to standardise interpretation of deterioration ratings via a forthcoming training initiative.

Moseley & District is satisfied with the use of site based inspections in order to create good costed plans of necessary replacement works at a time when they become necessary, as well as applying checks and balances to life-cycle costing analyses.

Moseley & District advocate the use of:

- a manageable lists of elements,
- varying life spans to incorporate usage by certain client groups
- regular liaison with the development department on the findings of life-cycle analysis

Case study 9
Profile of a small RSL

The Abbeyfields (Solihull) Society Ltd was formed in the mid 1960s and has five houses around the town of Solihull, situated on the southern fringe of Birmingham. There are two pairs of houses on two sites and a single detached house on a third site. One of the houses in one pair dates from the turn of the century and is sited in a conservation area, hence there are limitations on the changes that can be made externally. The single house dates from the 1930s. Accommodation is provided on the Abbeyfield pattern for about forty residents.

The houses are run by voluntary house committees for each house, with an executive committee which oversees the running of all five houses and considers the strategic implication of the operations. One current issue is the consideration of options relating to the future viability of the single detached house which, because it is difficult to adapt to provide en-suite accommodation, is becoming difficult to let.

The total annual income available to the Society from rents is approximately £190,000. In recent years an extensive programme of essential modernisation and upgrading of the houses has been undertaken. This has included the installation of stairlifts and a passenger lift, the fitting of communication call systems, the installing of replacement windows, kitchen refurbishment and the provision of additional en-suite accommodation. In spite of some financial support from the Housing Corporation for this work, the previously substantial cash reserves held by the Society have been depleted.

For regular maintenance work, it is estimated that the general requirement for all five houses amounts to approximately £25,000 per annum of which some £10,000 is required to maintain the operations within safety and health requirements.

The Society now sees the need to develop a business plan for the medium term. It recognises the need to incorporate into this plan on-going costs of maintenance and refurbishment, and would also like to include the replacement of white goods and other fittings and equipment within the houses. At the present time, annual budgets are developed and the working knowledge of individuals is used to ensure that these contain all the necessary elements for maintenance and refurbishment costs, although

often the perceived refurbishment needs cannot all be met in one financial year. It is felt that the Society could meet any expected maintenance demands, for example for a new roof, from its reserves.

There is currently no independent and systematic inspection of the condition of the properties, apart from that called for under health and safety requirements. The Society does however employ architects, structural engineers, and health and safety officers with professional indemnity insurance for any major structural repairs, and for any works which require Local Authority building and planning approvals. All these works are recorded on files and then passed on to other individuals, if necessary. The society also keeps files on each house indicating all other works carried out.

Appendix C
Reference section

The development of this guide
The Good Practice Guide to Maintenance Cost Forecasting: Project Report
Coventry University Enterprises, 1999

Business planning for RSLs
Manual of Housing Association Finance
CIPFA/National Housing Federation, 1998

Getting On or Getting By: Best Value and Registered Social Landlords: Conference Report
The Housing Corporation, 1998

Benchmarking Housing Performance: A Guide for RSLs
Aldbourne Associates and the Housing Corporation 1998

Financial Planning: A Practical Guide
National Housing Federation, 1996

Asset management and reinvestment
Reinvestment Strategies: A Good Practice Guide
National Housing Federation, 1997

Identification and prevention of anti-social behaviour
Safe as Houses: A Guide for Registered Social Landlords
Crime Concern, 1999

Commissioning maintenance work
Constructing the Team: Joint Review of Procurement and Contractual Arrangements in the United Kingdom Construction Industry: Final report
Sir Michael Latham, HMSO, 1994

Rethinking Construction: Report of the Construction Task Force to the Deputy Prime Minister
Sir John Egan, Department of the Environment, Transport and the Regions, HMSO, 1998

Energy efficiency
Energy Management for Affordable Warmth
A manual for Registered Social Landlords
People for Action and Chris Barnett Associates, People for Action, 1999

The Home Energy Conservation Act 1995 for Registered Social Landlords
NEA, 1997

Good Practice Briefing: Energy Efficiency
Chartered Institute of Housing, Issue 6, October 1996

Directory of Energy Efficient Housing
R. Lowe, M. Bell and D. Johnston, Chartered Institute of Housing, 1996

Standards and performance standards
Standards and Quality in Development
National Housing Federation, 1998

Performance Standards and Regulatory Guidance for Registered Social Landlords
The Housing Corporation, 1997

Stock condition surveys
Keeping Up Appearances: A Guide to Commissioning Stock Condition Surveys
London Housing Federation, 1998

Condition Surveys for Housing Associations
D. Marshall Construction Papers No 68 Chartered Institute of Building, 1996

Coding Standards for Stock Surveys and Repairs and Maintenance
National Federation of Housing Associations, 1996

State of Stock: Developing Effective Stock Condition Surveys
London Housing Federation 1996

Stock Condition Surveys: A Basic Guide for Housing Associations
National Federation of Housing Associations, 1994

Local House Condition Surveys
General Advice to Local Authorities
Department of the Environment – Building Research Establishment, HMSO, 1993

Techniques

Standards of Almshouse Management: A Guide to Good Practice
The Almshouse Association, 1998

Management Accounting (ZBB)
T. Lucy, DP Publications, (4th ed) 1996

Property Profiling and Data Collection for Housing Repairs and Improvements: Parts 1 & 2
R. Holmes, D Marshall and T. Butchers
Construction Papers Nos. 61 and 62, Chartered Institute of Building, 1996

Life Cycle Analysis of Housing
Scottish Homes – The National Housing Agency
Scottish Homes Working Paper 1996

Life-Cycle Cost Modelling
P. Gaskell-Taylor, NFHA and Joseph Rowntree Trust, Research Report No.7, 1989

Meaningless and Meaningful Maintenance Planning
A.A.J. Damen, NFHA and Joseph Rowntree Trust Research Report No 7, 1989

Performance of building components

Premature Failure of Building Components in Social Housing: Managing the Risk
R. Holmes and P. Wornell, Construction Paper No 46, Chartered Institute of Building, 1995

Obsolescence in Buildings: Data for Life-Cycle Costing
A. Ashworth, Construction Paper No 74, Chartered Institute of Building, 1995

Life Component Manual
Housing Association Property Mutual Ltd
E & FN Spon, 1992

BRE Life Expectancies of Building Components: Preliminary Results from a Survey of Building Surveyors' Views.
Royal Institute of Chartered Surveyors, Research Paper No. 11, 1992

Maintenance Cycles and Life Expectancies of Building Components and Materials: A Guide to Data and Sources
NBA Construction Consultants, 1985

General

Rents, Resources and Risks: The New balancing Act
National Housing Federation, 1997

Good Practice Briefing: Planned Maintenance and Improvements
Chartered Institute of Housing, Issue 9, 1997

Housing Quality Indicators: A Feasibility Study
Department of the Environment, Transport and the Regions 1997

Contract Practice for Surveyors
J.W. Ramus & S. Birchall, Laxtons (3rd ed), 1996

The Management of Risk
R. Fellows, Construction Papers No 65, Chartered Institute of Building, 1996

Methods of Forecasting Housing Maintenance Costs Employed by Housing Associations
M. Close, Coventry University, 1996

Long Term Maintenance: The Problems Facing Housing Associations
National Federation of Housing Associations, 1991

Improving Council House Maintenance
The Audit Commission, 1986